BETTER MARRIAGE

BETTER MARRIAGE

Against All Odds

Kendall and Starla Bridges

A BETTER MARRIAGE

PUBLISHED BY KENDALL BRIDGES MINISTRIES, CARROLLTON, TX

Unless otherwise noted, scripture quotations are taken from the HOLY BIBLE, NEW INTERNATIONAL VERSION®. Copyright © 1973, 1978, 1984 Biblica. Used by permission of Zondervan. Scripture quotations marked (MSG) are taken from *The Message*. Copyright © 1993, 1994, 1995, 1996, 2000, 2001, 2002. Used by permission of NavPress Publishing Group. Scripture quotations marked (NLV) are taken from the New Life Version. Copyright © Christian Literature International. Scripture quotations marked (NLT) are taken from the Holy Bible, New Living Translation, copyright ©1996, 2004, 2007, 2013, 2015 by Tyndale House Foundation. Used by permission of Tyndale House Publishers, Inc., Carol Stream, Illinois 60188. All rights reserved. Scripture quotations marked (AMP) are taken from the Amplified Bible, Copyright © 1954, 1958, 1962, 1964, 1965, 1987 by The Lockman Foundation. Used by permission. Scripture quotations marked (NKJV) are taken from the New King James Version®. Copyright © 1982 by Thomas Nelson. Used by permission. All rights reserved. Scripture quotations marked (ESV) are taken from the (The Holy Bible, English Standard Version), copyright © 2001 by Crossway Bibles, a publishing ministry of Good News Publishers. Used by permission. All rights reserved.

ISBN-13: 9780692754375

Cover Design: Dandy Bridges
Cover Photos: Andrew Lawhon
Cover photos shot on location at RE:defined Coffee House, Grapevine, TX
ISBN-10: 0692754377

Endorsements

"Kendall and Starla Bridges have written their testimony the way it should be written. Their story of faith, grace and redemption is written with clarity, honesty, passion and purpose. No life-changing truth is hidden from the reader. Their forthrightness will change the lives of all who journey with them toward a *Better Marriage – Against all Odds*. As you read this book, prepare to experience a transformation."

J. Don George
Pastor, Calvary Church
Irving, Texas

"What a testimony of grace and grit. If you are looking for a pretty, feel-good book then this may not be it. However, you have to look beyond the scars and discover a new beauty. There is beauty behind these ashes. This book will serve as dashboard indicators to us all. Way to go Starla and Kendall!! Thanks for being so thought provoking."

Mike D. Robertson
Pastor of Visalia First
Author of *Mind Viruses*
Visalia, California

"No words can describe the joy I have in reading this story I know so well. When I first met with Kendall and Starla after his failure, it appeared hopeless for restoration of any kind. But these two, committed to Christ and to each other, have been miraculously restored in their marriage and ministry. This is a compelling story of grace, mercy, forgiveness and love. Here is absolute proof there is hope after failure!"

Reverend Doug Fulenwider
Former Superintendent
Louisiana District of the Assemblies of God

"This book is the real life account of two people who faced the loss of everything that matters: family, friends and faith; and found a way to overcome it all and rebuild. This book will give hope to every married couple who reads it."

Doug McAllister
Author and Lead Pastor, Journey Fellowship Church
Lacombe, LA

"I know this couple. I know their kids. I have seen the new family, better family, they have become. I have seen the ministry they now lead and the people they are now able to touch. I have seen the victory they have forged out of the fire of destruction. And I'm glad they are bringing their story out into the public proving that the last word should always belong to God, not the devil. Learn from their failure but even more, learn from their victory! This book is a must read for every married person in America!"

Rick Dubose
District Superintendent
North Texas District of the Assemblies of God

"It's rare to find two people willing to be so brutally honest about their own pain. *Better Marriage – Against all Odds* is so much more than a story of brokenness. These pages contain tangible hope for people in desperate need of God's redeeming power. Read this book and be encouraged that God is able to bring beauty from brokenness."

John Lindell
Lead Pastor, James River Church
Springfield, MO
Jamesriver.org

"*Better Marriage – Against all Odds* is going to help so many marriages who are desperately reaching for hope. It's never easy to share a painful marriage story, but I'm so glad Kendall & Starla did!"

John McKinzie
Lead Pastor, Hope Fellowship
Frisco, TX
Hopefellowship.net

"Thank you, Kendall and Starla, for letting God use your story to bring healing to broken people and messed up marriages. *Better Marriage – Against All Odds* is a testimony of grace and redemption that reminds us that nothing is impossible for God."

Scott Wilson
Senior Pastor, The Oaks Fellowship
Red Oak, TX
Author of *Clear the Stage: Making Room for God*

"This book, this heartfelt delivery of a real life experience and truth, will help you avoid the same pain yourself, and will help you discover your way back from brokenness! Kendall & Starla Bridges are friends and colleagues in ministry, and I am thrilled to recommend "*Better Marriage!*""

Maury Davis
Senior Pastor, Cornerstone Church
Nashville, Tennessee

Kolt, Kanon, Londyn, Laura, Maverick, Hunter, Kendall, Starla, Summer, Mase, Tyler, Sarah, River and Dandy

Kolt, Summer, Kendall, Starla, Hunter and Dandy

Dedication

We would like to dedicate this book to our four beautiful children: Kendall Kolt, Dandy Sterling, Summer Star and Hunter Sky. You are gifts from God to us. We treasure every moment God gives us with you here on this earth. You make life so much fun, exciting and meaningful.

Our lives are full and complete because of each one of you. You are each one the perfect ingredient to make our family exactly what God intended for it to be. We know that your strength and support made it possible for us to survive this terrible storm.

We did it! We made it through that which seemed impossible.

You walked this entire journey with us. Your love, your courage and encouragement were such a vital part of our healing.

We came through stronger, closer and better than before.

We are beyond blessed that God allowed us to be your parents.

Our story is not over, the miracle continues...

God has blessed our family with more wonderful children. Kolt is married to a beautiful woman of God named Laura. Dandy is married to a beautiful woman of God named Sara. Summer Star is married to a handsome man of God named Tyler. Hunter Sky's man is on the way. Thank you kids for making our family better.

We love you!
Momma and Daddy

Foreword

George O. Wood
General Superintendent
The Assemblies of God

I've long been intrigued by the Apostle Paul's comments in 2 Corinthians 3:13, *We are not like Moses, who would put a veil over his face to keep the Israelites from gazing at it while the radiance was fading away.*

Imagine this scenario. Moses' face was radiantly bright because of his encounter with God – so bright that the people couldn't look at him. It was before sunglasses! To deal with the problem, Moses put a veil on.

One day when he got up he looked in the mirror at himself and thought, "Hmm. I don't seem as bright today as I was yesterday." But, he put the veil back on anyway. Day by day, as he got up, he would look in the mirror and each day he was a little less bright. Finally, the day came when his face was ordinary again – no special glow, no outstanding radiance.

He had a decision to make. "Do I let the people know I'm normal, or do I keep up appearances?" As righteous a man as he was, he decided to fake it. He wouldn't let the people know that the glow had faded away.

His dilemma is a lot like some of the decisions we make – between our public and our private face, or as I would identify it – between our person and our persona.

We who are in vocational ministry especially face this issue all the time. We can easily fall into the trap of carrying on a dichotomy between what we are in the pulpit and who we are at home; who we are in carrying out the responsibilities of ministry (our *persona*) and who we are at home (our *person*).

The Apostle Paul says the cure for this is to take off the veil – to present ourselves in such a way that people can see we are being "transformed into His likeness with every increasing glory." In other words, we need to be so real that people can see us actually becoming more like Christ. They can watch our progress rather than our playing the game of religiosity by appearing to be something we are not.

Kendall and Starla Bridges have captured this vital perspective in their own lives and marriage through the harrowing personal journey they walked. This book is filled with transparency and honesty as they tell their story of passage through the nightmare of infidelity into the sunlight of transparency and healing.

It's a whole lot easier to fall down than to get up. Try it. Go ahead and fall down, then try to pick yourself up. See what takes more effort. My admiration goes to Kendall and Starla. Yes, they fell down – but they didn't stay down. With God's help, great counsel, and a will to forgive, they got up. And, like Job, today they are in far better shape than when the sorrow began.

But their story is not one just for ministers or those who are in troubled marriages. It's jammed with sound Biblical counsel for any married couple. This book will help strengthen your marriage and give you sound principles on which to build "a better marriage against all odds." I commend this book to you!

George O. Wood
General Superintendent
The Assemblies of God

Contents and Chapters

Acknowledgments

"IT TOOK A VILLAGE"

"Thank you for touching my life in ways you never knew. My riches do not lie in material wealth but in having friends like you."

— UNKNOWN AUTHOR

We want to take the opportunity to express our gratitude to the people who helped make this restoration possible. The best kinds of people in this world are the ones that God sends into your life—the ones who make you see the sun where you once saw darkness. They're the people that believe in you so much that you start to believe in yourself too. They are the ones who refuse to turn their backs on you.

They're the people who walk through the storm with you, pray with you, and believe in your dreams, your miracles, and your restoration. They love you in the good times and the bad. They are "once in a lifetime" kind of people, whom we lovingly call family and friends.

To you we say, "Thank You!"

First, and above all, thank You, God, for paying the price that we might be forgiven, for healing our marriage and our family, and for restoring our ministry. Thank you for giving us the courage to fight the fight and for making us *better*!

To James and Joyce Bridges & John and Vivian McDuff (our parents):
We are more than blessed to have such wonderful, godly examples of parents in our lives. You have no idea how much the sacrifices you made throughout our lives has

resulted in us finding strength to fight for a *better marriage*. Thank you for staying, loving, praying, counseling, financially blessing, and believing in us! Because of you, we are stronger and better. Thank you for showing us how to love God and how to love each other. Thank you Momma (Vivian) for teaching us to always, always trust God. Thank you Daddy (John) for teaching us to always show mercy. Thank you Mom (Joyce) for teaching us to live life to the fullest. Thank you Dad (James) for teaching us to seek wisdom. You exemplified Christ!

John D and Kelli McDuff...My sweet big brother and sister. Your counsel, your love, and your example have always encouraged me to live like Christ. I love you, brother bear. I miss you, my sweet sister. (Starla)

Dr. Richard D. Dobbins (Doc)...You're in heaven now, but I believe God has given you a glimpse of the countless lives you've changed. Your counsel was so rich, godly, and spot on! You always knew what to say. Thank you, thank you, thank you!

Dr. George O. Wood...Thank you for your phone calls. You spoke life to us, encouraged us, and refused to give up on us. You didn't have to allow us into this program. Thank you for giving us a second chance. We are proud to call you our General Superintendent. Your wisdom and vision and compassion is very much appreciated. We believe in you; thank you for believing in us.

Superintendent Doug Fulenwider and the Louisiana District...For going far above what you were supposed to do in our restoration. Your love and counsel were life changing!

Superintendent Rick and Rita DuBose and the North Texas District...For welcoming us back home, taking a chance on us, believing in us, and investing in us as we launched into pastoring again.

Superintendent Joe Granberry and Superintendent Howard Burroughs...For going out of your way to get us started on this road of restoration.

Pastor J. Don and Gwen George and Calvary Church...For welcoming us into your church, including us in your family, and for loving our girls. For investing in our future and pushing us out of the "nest," back into ministry, and for encouraging us to fly.

Daddy Jack and Momma Carole Pruitt...For taking us in as your own children. For the groceries, the donuts, the financial blessings, but most of all, the love and prayers.

Kerry and Valerie Jones...Thank you for believing in us, loving us, and encouraging us again and again.

Garry and Ann Page...For being true friends who loved us, cried with us, and made us laugh.

Richard and Lori Joy (our dearest friends)...You loved and stayed when we had nothing to give, no hope for the future, no reason to smile. We were in the pit, and you refused to turn your back on us. Thank you for encouraging us to write this book and for pushing us off the ledge to make it happen.

Deborah Hartman...For not letting me go under!

Fred Martinez...For being a friend who was as close as a brother D.F.M. I won't forget you!

Pastor Don Yandell...For countless calls, cards, encouragement, and gifts of love. You never missed an opportunity to bless our family.

Pastors Doug and Rachel McAllister...When God told you to be our friends, you had no idea we would be this much trouble. But we sure needed you. We love you guys!

Pastors Greg and Kristie Hollis...Thank you for believing in us and supporting us month after month. Oh yeah, and for allowing us to come minister in your church, even though you didn't show up. Ha!

Dr. Randy Hurst...For believing in us month after month after month. What a friend!

Pastor Maury and Gail Davis...You believed in us, encouraged us, and helped us with much-needed support to launch Freedom Church. You entrusted your church and your children to us. We are humbled and honored.

Pastor Carl and Cindy Richard and Glad Tidings Church...For taking in and loving a very broken family.

Pastor John and Debbie Lindell...Thank you, Friend. You were willing to take us in. You gave us much needed love and support, and you and James River will always have a special place in our hearts.

Pastor Mike and Karen Robertson...Thanks for your friendship, support, and the great ideas we have stolen.

Pastor John and Melissa McKinzie...Thanks for being a friend, going to lunch with me, and for just being there.

Marcus and Joni Lamb...For sending your gift of love and encouraging words. You didn't know us, but you invested in us anyway.

Robby and Vanessa McGee...We want to say thank you to this very special couple for taking the time to handle the details of making this book happen (you know I hate details, KB). Thanks for pushing it across the finish line. It wouldn't have happened without you.

Mike and Heidi Jonker...Thank you to two very selfless people who took the time to proof and edit this book. You were willing to pour through the pages again and again. Thank you. I owe you many Starbucks gift cards!

Joel and Jamie Perkins...Thank you guys for your friendship. We are so sorry that we put you in such a difficult position, yet you continued to love.

Thank you to the pastors and friends who took a chance on us, allowing us to minister after we returned to ministry:

Pastor Jacob and Michelle Aranza
Dr. James Barnes
Pastor Matthew Barnett
Pastor Tommy Barnett
Pastor John and Shelli Bates
Dr. Kermit and Jan Bridges S.A.G.U.
Pastor Duane Brogdon
Apostle Paul J. and Maxine Butler
Pastor Randy and Debbie Carter
Pastor Mike and Tammy Comiskey
Pastor Denny and DeAnza Duron
Pastor Al and Marla Eden
Pastor Armando Garcia
Pastor J. Don and Gwen George
Pastor Andy and Cheryl Harris
Pastor Lonnie Huett
Pastor Roger Hoffpowier
Pastors Greg and Kristie Hollis
Pastor Kason and April Huddleston
Pastor Bryan and Haley Jarrett
Pastor Ron and Sandy Johnson
Pastor Elwyn and ReGina Johnston
Pastor Richard and Lori Joy
Pastor Roy Love
Pastors Doug and Rachel McAllister
Dr. John D. and Kelli McDuff
Pastor Alan and Shelley Neel
Pastor Goodluck and Angela Okotie-eboh
Pastor Richard and Ladonna Plunk
Pastor Carl and Cindy Richard

Pastor Jacob Rodriguez
Pastor Dan and Bonnie Scheaffer
Pastor Greg and Rosalind Simien
Pastor Ben and Beth Terry
Pastor Valentino D. Williams
Pastor Don and Debbie Yandell

You are all lifesavers to us. We are indebted to you for the kindness you showed and the opportunities you gave. Thank you! We pray this prayer over you.

Philippians 1:3-11 *says, "3 I thank my God every time I remember you. 4 In all my prayers for all of you, I always pray with joy 5 because of your partnership in the gospel from the first day until now, 6 being confident of this, that He who began a good work in you will carry it on to completion until the day of Christ Jesus. 7 It is right for me to feel this way about all of you, since I have you in my heart and, whether I am in chains or defending and confirming the gospel, all of you share in God's grace with me. 8 God can testify how I long for all of you with the affection of Christ Jesus. 9 And this is my prayer: that your love may abound more and more in knowledge and depth of insight, 10 so that you may be able to discern what is best and may be pure and blameless for the day of Christ, 11 filled with the fruit of righteousness that comes through Jesus Christ—to the glory and praise of God."*

Kendall and Starla Bridges

Introduction

The night begins with a nice dinner out with a new couple you've just met. Everything seems to be going smoothly, but then you hear it. The question is asked that you were hoping wouldn't come up: "So, you planted and pastored a successful church in Houston, Texas, for fifteen years, and then you left there, moved to another city, and started all over again from nothing. Why? What were you thinking? Why in the world would you do that? What's your story?"

I can't tell you how many times we've heard that question. At first, we would squirm around in our seats, start to sweat, and feel that heat flash of awkward embarrassment rushing through our bodies. You know the one—like when your teacher or, even worse, your pastor (who in both of our cases was our father), calls you down for talking in front of the whole congregation. There may be only hundreds looking, but at that moment it feels like thousands. Yeah, *that* feeling.

We look at each other and say with our eyes, "Tag, you're it! You tell them." We would then begin to unveil our story layer by ugly, painful layer.

It has gotten easier through the years, not because it's something we are proud of. Nope! It would have been so much easier to get through it, past it, and pretend it never happened.

However, God made it very clear to us that "our story" was to be used to help others. It's easier because we see how much it has encouraged others. They, too, can make it. They, too, can have a restored marriage. They, too, can make what seems bad, ugly, impossible, and hopeless so much better than they ever thought possible! We are here to tell *you*, "Better is worth the fight!"

John 10:10 says, *"The thief comes only to steal and kill and destroy; I have come that they may have life, and have it to the full."*

Did you notice in the scripture above it says, "The thief *only* comes to steal, kill, and destroy?" Satan's purpose is death and destruction. That's it and nothing else. But Jesus has come to bring us life—not just a mundane life that we barely get through, but life to the full! *The Message Bible* says it this way, "I came so they can have real and eternal life, more and better life than they ever dreamed of." Do you want death and destruction, or life better than you've ever dreamed of? Choose Jesus...choose life...choose better!

Since "What's your story?" seems to be the question we've heard hundreds of times in the last several years, we decided to tell our story. It's not pretty; it's uncomfortable, but it is who we are. Everyone has a story, but not everyone is willing to remove the veil and tell it.

In the pages ahead, you will hear our story told from both sides. Our styles are different, but our story is the same. Then we'll come together to help encourage you to build a better marriage by giving you practical steps to take in order to live out the marriage God intended for you to have.

Our desire, our goal, our purpose is to help others. Believe us, we take no personal joy from sharing our ugliest moments as a couple, but there is great joy in knowing that in some small way we have helped someone know that they are not alone. There is hope for a better marriage, and you will get through this one step, one day, and one victory at a time.

Get a hot cup of coffee or tea. Come sit down across the table from us, and let us tell you our story.

Part 1:
Starla's Chapters 1-10

1

(Starla)
Fairytale Schmairytale

All little girls, even the ones who start out tomboys like me, grow up with a false imagination of what love and marriage is all about. After slaying dragons and a wicked queen, the handsome prince (the knight in shining armor) rides in on a muscular stallion to save the princess (the damsel in distress). They get married, rule their kingdom, and live happily ever after. Lies!

I was born into a loving family. I was the fourth child. My parents had three boys and then me, their long-awaited girl. Sounds like trouble already, right? I pretty much got whatever I wanted.

I had stringy fine hair, wore glasses (four eyes), freckled, loved to climb trees like a monkey, and played sports more than I did with dolls. Get the picture? My "awkward stage" seemed much longer than everyone else's. Nonetheless, I was still a little princess in my momma and daddy's eyes.

I never doubted my parents' love for me. They raised me well and always encouraged me and told me how beautiful I was. Still, I never felt pretty. I didn't feel like I measured up to what the world saw as beautiful. I didn't hate my life. In fact, I loved it! I just had low self-esteem.

My parents pastored a church my entire life. I lived in a fish bowl with a revolving door of friends coming and going. So I decided early on to put walls up so people couldn't hurt me.

I grew up faster than most and traveled as a music artist in the early '80s. God quickly blessed my music with airtime and concerts, but I didn't really enjoy traveling alone or entertaining. It was a bit empty for me.

I didn't enjoy school very much, so when I finally finished, I was ecstatic! Then, out of the blue, for some strange reason I decided to attend Bible college. That happened on a Sunday, and I was enrolled by the following Wednesday. WHAT?

As soon as I finished my paperwork, it hit me. I had been sabotaged by God to be there. Remember, I didn't like school! (If you're a teacher reading this, I am so sorry.)

I met a guy within the first week of classes in August of 1981. We ended up in the same circle of friends. Neither one of us was interested in having a relationship at the time, so we felt very safe hanging out together. Before we knew it, most of our other friends faded out of the picture, and we were spending our free time together. We became best of friends.

Then, out of nowhere, we kissed. He walked back to his car; I walked into the dorm, and we were both in shock. Where did that come from? What just happened? By the following February, we were engaged, and in August of the next year, we were married. I was nineteen. He was twenty-one. So, this was the reason God "tricked" me in to going to school.

AN UNHEALTHY START

I believe we are attracted to our opposite personality type because God knows exactly who we need to complete us. He knows who we need to accomplish the assignments He has for us. Kendall and I were very different from each other.

Kendall was the confident, handsome prince with a positive outlook on every-thing. A dreamer with no desire to work through details to get what he wanted. He trusted everyone and was hardheaded.

Starla, the cute, chubby princess, had very little confidence, doubted herself, and trusted no one. She saw the negative in unplanned dreams and all of the things that could go wrong. She was hardheaded.

Rather than embrace the differences that were placed there by God to make us stronger together as a team than we ever could have been alone, we tried to change each other. We started dwelling on the weaknesses of our differences instead of developing the strengths that would make us a force to be reckoned with.

It's not our job to change each other. It's our job to ask God to show us our own weaknesses and to help us become the people He created us to be.

Kendall and I were still friends and thought we were happy. We bought into the lie of "agree to disagree," but that doesn't resolve the issues. That only creates a snowball of disaster ahead. There will always be things you don't agree on. Work through the important ones, and forget about the silly things that just don't matter. Choose your battles wisely.

Years of continuing to live this way put a wedge in our relationship. We still had fun together; however, the chord of unity was slowly being torn apart. It was growing weaker and weaker.

WE LOVED WRONG

Kendall loved himself more than he loved me. He lived to build his ministry and elevate his platform, and I didn't love him completely. I wasn't an encourager. Instead of working with him to make his dreams a reality, I crushed Kendall's ideas. Remember the "guarded-heart girl" who didn't trust anyone? I wasn't about to let him have all of my love. I had to guard myself—just in case.

In the first 10 years of our marriage, we had four children. We were youth pastors for six years and then pioneered a church. We were living two different lives. I was a full-time mommy. Kendall was a full-time pastor. We were still a decent team, just not a united, winning one. The weaknesses in our character took over.

I became a calloused, wicked queen who wanted no one to enter her kingdom. Kendall became the evil dragon that breathed fire and destroyed everything in his path. Eventually, our self-built kingdom crumbled.

HAPPILY EVER AFTER

The mistake we made from day one was building our own kingdom and not the kingdom of God.

The mistake we made from day one was building our own kingdom and not the kingdom of God. We were trying to build a marriage that measured up to the world's standards, not His. We looked great on the outside, but we were crumbling on the inside. Our house was built on sand, and it ultimately led to complete destruction.

Even so, God turned into good what was meant for evil. He brought us to this new position we have today, using our story to help others (**Genesis 50:20** paraphrased). God has done miraculous things in our marriage, and we can't keep silent. We have a "happily ever after" that doesn't end here on earth. It will last throughout eternity.

Simplified

The reality is no marriage is like a fairytale, but marriage can, and should, be beautiful! A perfect marriage is two imperfect people who refuse to give up on each other and who surrender everything completely to a perfect God.

Our priorities are now in order: God, marriage, family, and ministry (or job). We love with a love that God intended, an unselfish love. I am more in love with Kendall today than ever before. He is my perfectly imperfect prince charming. This is way better than any fairytale!

2

(Starla)
TSUNAMI

Sunday December 26th, 2004—the day after Christmas, *Boxing Day*. Thousands of people were enjoying what seemed to be another beautiful day in paradise. Many were on Christmas holiday along the Indian Ocean beaches. Others were going about their normal daily routines. Then suddenly, without warning, their lives forever changed.

There was an underwater earthquake, registering 9.1 on the Richter scale. It was equivalent to approximately 550 million times the atomic bomb dropped on Hiroshima. Waves that hit the state of Sumatra, Indonesia, were recorded at 80-100 feet tall, and the damage continued all the way to the Indian Ocean.

Altogether, an estimated 230,000 to 260,000 people died. The Indian Ocean tsunami was the most deadly in recorded history. I watched many of the videos that tourists shot just prior to the wave coming in. They knew things were odd, or "not right," as they watched the tide retreat far back in to the sea, leaving boats on dry land.

Instead of running for safety, they were drawn toward the danger. They took pictures and shot videos, so they could show their friends and family what they witnessed. They were fascinated by the strange phenomenon.

This is so much like the attack of satan. He lures us into something "different." We know it's not normal; we know it's not right. Instead of fleeing for safety, we are drawn closer. The wave then hits without warning, and we've gone in too far to escape. We run as fast as we can. Some of us get out of the way of danger just in time. Others make it through with only a few scrapes and bruises. Many refuse to give up and are determined to find something to hold on to. They will not let go! Then there are others who aren't strong enough, who just can't seem to keep their heads above water. They let go. They give up. They lose the battle.

Psalm 93:3-4 says, *"The mighty oceans have roared, O Lord. The mighty oceans roar like thunder, the mighty oceans roar as they pound the shore. 4 But mightier than the violent raging of the seas, mightier than the breakers on the shore—the Lord above is mightier than these!" (NLT)*

Yes, the ocean is powerful, and so are the attacks of satan. But our God is mightier than any of these! Always remember this.

DECEMBER 2004

Sitting in a small duplex, in a different town, in a different state, I was uprooted from everything I knew to be "home." I was scrolling through hundreds of pictures on my computer of the devastating effects from the 2004 Indian Ocean tsunami. I saw unrecognizable piles of debris that used to be people's houses, belongings, businesses, and lives. I saw thousands of bodies stacked on top of each other. The healthy reaction of seeing scenes like this would be to feel heartbroken for them and their families, but I found myself wishing I could trade places with them. Dead to the world, and dead to the pain of what lay ahead.

"They are the lucky ones," I thought. Their fear and pain only lasted for a few moments. They don't have to look in the eyes of their children and try to explain why this happened. They don't have to rebuild their entire life again because everything they owned and everything they've ever known had been completely stripped away. They are free!

I realize this may seem a little extreme to some of you reading this, but this is how I felt, and I want to be completely open and honest with you. I was depressed and devastated. I was crushed and had no feelings of hope whatsoever.

I've been in the ministry my entire life, grew up in it, and married into it. It's all I've ever known. I was married to my college sweetheart of twenty-one years. We had four beautiful children—two boys, two girls. We were pastoring a successful, fast-growing church that we started in our home fifteen years prior. Our outward appearance was "the perfect family with the perfect life." I loved my family, our church, and my life, but I knew a storm was coming. All the signs were there. Regardless of my warnings, my prayers, my pleading, there was nothing I could do to stop it. My tsunami was headed straight for me, and all I could do was hold on, brace myself for impact, and try to save my children.

My tsunami was headed straight for me, and all I could do was hold on, brace myself for impact, and try to save my children.

We live in fear of that which we think we can't survive. This was the one thing I thought would destroy me. In May of 2004, the full-blown storm finally hit. My husband had been unfaithful. His secret was out. No more hiding, no more lying, no more denying my accusations. He was exposed and, in a strange way, I was at peace. The heavy load I was carrying alone was revealed, and I could finally get help.

Although my "perfect" world was crumbling and my future was completely unknown, I no longer felt like I was losing my mind. When a person is living in sin and they know it, the more they are accused or questioned the angrier they become. They put blame on everyone and everything else. They play the victim, attack the accuser, and defend themselves.

There had been so many heated arguments in our home. The deeper my husband got into sin, the angrier he became with me. He blamed the tension in our marriage on me: "Some pastor's wife I was! I didn't trust him the way I should. I needed to get in control of my thoughts. I was being very selfish and ungodly."

I heard it so much that I started to believe him. Maybe I was completely wrong. Maybe I was being ungodly and was the one with the problem. Maybe I'm about to blow it and lose my family because of my accusations, my jealousy, and my insecurities. I was exhausted. I didn't have it in me to fight anymore. Things were too far-gone.

So here's where the "strange but welcomed peace" came into the picture. I wasn't crazy. My discernment had been correct. I was hearing what God was telling me. Now that the sin is exposed, I can move on to the next chapter of life…whatever that may be.

When I was completely shattered, I searched for anything and everything that could help me. Honestly, all I wanted was to hear from others who had been through what I was going through.

I wanted their advice. I wanted to know that what I was feeling was normal. I wanted to know how they got through this. As far as I was concerned, if people had not walked in my shoes, they had no idea what I was feeling and really couldn't help.

Let me throw in a little advice here. If you want to help people going through a crisis, don't preach to them. Don't tell them you understand if you've never experienced what they are experiencing. Don't tell them what they "could have done differently" to prevent this from happening, and don't try to fix them. You can't! They need a faithful friend to listen, love, encourage, pray, and remain until long after the storm passes.

My purpose in sharing my story with you is not to give details of my husband's sin, but to tell you about our healing journey. My prayer is that our words, will give you a hope for your future and restoration. My sincere desire is that our story can prevent others from experiencing this pain. I want you to see the affect sin had, not only in our marriage, but also on our children, our family, and our friends. The act of sin is selfish, but the ripple effect goes farther than we will ever know.

You've likely heard it said, "Sin will take you further than you want to go, keep you longer than you want to stay, and cost you more that you want to pay," yet we still give in to the temptation of sin daily.

Psalm 1:6 says, "For the Lord watches over the path of the godly, but the way of the wicked leads to destruction." (NLT)

Proverbs 16:18 says, "Pride goes before destruction, and haughtiness before a fall." (NLT)

Romans 6:20-21 says, "When you're a slave to sin, the result is living in shame and a life that ends in eternal doom. It destroys you and has the potential to destroy all of those around you." (Paraphrased)

Simplified

The destruction of my husband's sin was larger than he ever could have imagined.

It completely wiped out everything our family had built over twenty-one years. We had to start over again from nothing. I couldn't imagine the possibility of ever getting better, but wait, the story is just beginning.

3

(Starla)

VERTIGO

Have you ever experienced vertigo? I have, and let me tell you, it is crazy weird. In a moment, a slight turn of the head, you feel like you are being jerked around from left to right, whirling around, up, down, and all around in circles. It can take you down flat to the ground in seconds. All you can do is lay there, close your eyes, wait, and pray it passes quickly. This is how I would describe the emotions I went through after I heard the truth about my husband's secret life.

When I got the phone call from him that he had been found out or busted, he was in a bad way. I guess he was experiencing his own vertigo. He went from telling me he had been unfaithful to, "I'm going to end my life. It will be better for everyone." I went from wanting to kill him to having to save his life.

The atmosphere felt like there had been a death in the family, and in a way, that's exactly what had happened.

I was angry, angrier than I ever thought possible for me. Honestly, I felt like I could kill him. If he had been standing in front of me, I'm pretty sure I could have done some bodily harm. But my desire to "fix him" kicked in long enough for me to calmly call my two boys, who were young adults at the time. I had them start calling their father's phone. I thought if he could see their names appear on his caller ID, even if he didn't answer their calls, he would be forced to think about someone other than himself. I even talked to him off and on those first several hours. With God's help, I was able to say what he needed to hear and not what I was feeling.

Kendall came home that evening. By this time, the house was full of our family, close friends, and leaders from our church. The atmosphere felt like there had been a death in the family, and in a way, that's exactly what had happened.

I couldn't even look at him, and I sure couldn't talk to him. I could barely breathe. I honestly didn't care what he was thinking, saying, or feeling. His well-being was not registering on my radar. My job of getting him home alive was done. I left him in the care of the others, while I tried to wrap my head around the question, "What now?" I could barely handle one breath at a time.

FIVE STAGES OF GRIEF
DENIAL – ANGER – BARGAINING – DEPRESSION – ACCEPTANCE

I experienced each one of these. It's natural, and it's normal to feel these emotions of pain and grief. It's needed in your healing process, but when the grief takes over your life and you feel hopeless, helpless, and worthless, you're in too far. I walked my healthy portion of these stages, but then I took it too far. I set up camp and stayed in my misery. (I'll talk more about that later.)

DENIAL

Even though I knew my husband had been unfaithful, I wished I could wake up from the nightmare. I so desperately didn't want it to be true. I didn't want to go through this valley of darkness. I had already been there before with my father.

I knew the years of pain, embarrassment, and rebuilding that were ahead for my children and me.

I knew some people would never forget and that we would be forever marked in their minds.

ANGER

Yes, I was angry. I didn't even know that I was capable of the levels of anger that I experienced. And honestly, it was scary! There may or may not have been objects thrown and a few slaps to a face. I was so angry with Kendall. How could he be so stupid? How could he throw away everything? All of the lies, all of the hateful things he said to our kids and me—I was "danger level" angry.

I was angry because I knew what people would be saying about me: "It takes two. It's never one-sided. She didn't meet his needs at home. If she would have only..." (You can fill in your own conclusion here. I'm sure you've done it before; I certainly had).

The problem wasn't that I failed to love him. I loved him wrong. I loved him the way I should only love God. I adored him, or worshiped him, if you will.

I was angry with God. I was mad because He didn't answer my prayers when I cried out to keep my husband from straying. He apparently didn't "have my back." Why didn't He stop this?

I was angry with our church leaders for punishing our whole family. Why did we all have to suffer for my husband's sin? (They did what they needed to do, but I was still mad.) It hurt when the people we had been working with for years said they needed to cut all ties with us.

I could so vividly remember the joys, struggles, and valleys we had walked through with each one of them. It was now our valley, and I felt like we had to walk it alone. So we did. We left and began the very long process of starting over.

BARGAINING

I told God how He should fix this: "Just let me die! That will fix things for me. Come on, God, I deserve that at least. You didn't rescue me before, so this would be a great way for you to make it up to me. Let Kendall stay here and deal with all the ugly." God obviously didn't accept my plan.

DEPRESSION

Yep, full on depression took over and controlled me.

Funny story: At our first counseling session, our counselor had us fill out a checklist of symptoms. He came out after reading them and told me I was depressed. Duh, really? How many years of schooling did that take you? My MDCS—Master's Degree in Common Sense—could have told you that (sarcastic moment over).

I honestly had no desire to live at all, but I wasn't suicidal. I just pleaded with God to take my life. I was paralyzed, numb to the core. I was convinced my kids would be better off without me. I had nothing to give. I wanted to love; I wanted to feel again, but I just couldn't. The desire was there, but the nerves were damaged and it would take a miracle for me to feel again.

There were times that I would hear myself gasp for a breath because I was in such a numb state that I would literally forget to breathe. I wasn't eating or drinking. I was dehydrated, and my weight dropped under a hundred pounds. At one point, someone rubbed my back, and I didn't even feel it. Seriously, I did not feel it.

I knew I had to get a grip, wake up, and try to live again, not for me but for my children. I couldn't think about the future. I just had to take it moment by moment, one breath at a time. Anything beyond that seemed impossible.

I had always heard the description "broken heart," but I never knew how real it was until mine was broken. The pain was like no pain I've ever experienced. It actually felt shredded, like it had been put through a meat grinder. The weight on my chest seemed unbearable. I didn't know if I could bounce back, but I was willing to try.

Psalm 34:18 says, "The Lord is close to the brokenhearted: He rescues those whose spirits are crushed." (NLT)

I saturated myself in the book of Psalms. It was my antidote for depression. It was life to me. I spent hours upon hours in my closet to grieve, read, or lie in silence—just Jesus and me. It was safe there. I didn't "feel" like praising. I didn't "feel" like praying, but I did it anyway. It was the only way for me to have any sort of life, peace, hope, and strength. I knew I couldn't walk this journey without God.

On June 16, 2004, I read the following from Psalms.

Psalm 42:1, 3-5, 8 "1 As the deer pants for streams of water, so I long for You, O God. 3 Day and night I have only tears for food, while my enemies continually taunt me, saying, "Where is this God of yours?" 4 My heart is breaking as I remember how it used to be: I walked among the crowds of worshipers, leading a great procession to the house of God, singing for joy and giving thanks it was the sound of a great celebration! 5 Why am I discouraged? Why so sad? I will put my hope in God! I will praise Him again—my Savior… 8 Through each day the Lord pours His unfailing love upon me, and through each night I sing His songs, praying to God who gives me life." (NLT)

ACCEPTANCE

I realized I had a choice. I could live in depression for the rest of my life and remain miserable, or accept my loss and do whatever it took to be restored and move on. I was wounded deeply and had to face battles in my mind every single day. I had to work through the "trigger things" (words, places, names, memories) that would break me. They still affect me to this day.

I knew I would forever have that sting of death in my heart—the death of my marriage and of broken vows, the death of a one-sided commitment. I also knew that if I didn't get up and fight, it would destroy me, and there would be no hope of being victorious. My healing would be a very long, slow process, but at least it was finally beginning.

Simplified

Going through the stages of grief is not only needed, it's necessary. But remaining in the stages of grief will destroy you.

Make sure to stay in the presence of God while you are on this journey. God understands a broken heart like no other, and He wants to heal yours.

Psalm 147:3 *says, "He heals the brokenhearted, and binds up their wounds." (NLT)*

He wants to make you better.

4

(Starla)

DIFFERENT

Affairs are devastating to everyone involved. After broken vows, every marriage will struggle; some will never recover. Families are torn apart. It shakes the foundation of your kids and causes them to lose the ability to trust.

When ministers have affairs (or sin), you pay an even higher price (if you follow the instructions in God's word on restoration for leaders). Not only do you experience the normal repercussions of an affair, you lose your platform, job, income, home, insurance, and purpose. You have to find a new way of living. You have to start completely over.

James 3:1 says, "For we who teach will be judged by God with greater strictness." *(Paraphrased)*

EXPECTATIONS OF A LEADER

Titus 1:6-9 says, "6 An elder must well thought of for his good life. He must be faithful to his wife, and his children must be believers who are not wild or rebellious. 7 An elder must live a blameless life because he is God's minister. He must not be arrogant or quick-tempered; he must not be a heavy drinker, violent, or greedy for money. 8 He must enjoy having guests in his home and must love all that is good. He must live wisely and be fair. He must live a devout and disciplined life. 9 He must have a strong and steadfast belief in the trustworthy message he was taught; then he will be able to encourage others with right teaching and show those who oppose it where they are wrong." (NLT)

God holds leaders to higher standards, but why? Because our calling is to lead people to Christ by living a godly example.

1 Timothy 5:20 says, "Anyone who sins should be rebuked in front of the whole church so that others will have a proper fear of God." *(NLT)*

In May of 2004, we stood before our congregation a very broken and hurting family. I will never forget that day and the way I felt. Here's what I wrote in my journal on that Sunday.

SUNDAY, MAY 23, 2004

The hardest ride of my life. Tonight we had to drive to the church and face our beautiful people and let them know that my husband, their pastor, had failed.

My body is weak, and I'm dehydrated. My heart is crushed and in so much pain. I feel like I have 500 pounds of pressure on my chest. I'm having a hard time breathing, and I'm sick to my stomach.

We arrived at 6:00 – the people were all seated waiting. We went straight to the backstage area and waited for the board to announce what had happened.

My mother and sister-in-law, Kelli, were there to give me much needed support.

My heart hurt so much for my four beautiful children, who had to face the congregation. It wasn't their fault. My heart hurt for all of our people. I didn't want them to turn their backs on God. It wasn't His fault.

My boys held me and were ready to catch me if I fell. No one wanted to walk on that platform. When they called us out, there was a jam at the door; no one wanted to be first. I took a deep breath, tried to hold my shoulders up, and walked out first.

As we entered, there was no music, just silence. Then the congregation stood as if they were watching a casket go by. That's just how it felt—there had been a death in our family. Then they began weeping. They, too, were heart broken.

I begged them not to turn their backs on God. He didn't fail them; man did.

First, my husband confessed his sin and asked forgiveness. To be honest, I didn't even listen to him. I couldn't even stand next to him. I did not want to hear what he had to say. My heart was only with my children and my people. Then they gave me the microphone, and I shared what I was feeling.

I was strong until I locked eyes with people. I saw tears and broken hearts, anger and confusion. It was so painful to see. I would feel myself start to break, then take a deep breath, and continue. I had to look above their heads so I could go on.

I begged them not to turn their backs on God. He didn't fail them; man did. I told them they had to make a choice, and I was choosing to be stronger and to put my complete trust and hope in God, and Him alone.

It was one of the hardest things I've ever done. The saddest part was that my children had to experience it all and feel the pain. No child should ever have to go through that.

UPROOTED

I became a prisoner in my home to save the embarrassment of running into people I knew or who knew me. We had been on local Christian television, and our church was well known in the area, so everywhere we went people recognized us.

Within three months of my husband's sin being exposed, we sold our home, sold most of our belongings, turned in our cars, packed up a truck, and moved to another state to try to start over. Kendall took a job making less than 30% of what he was making before. On top of the turmoil of pain, we had very little income to function. The only way we made it financially was with the help of a few friends and our parents.

Because this was a very public exposure, my children knew everything. My family split. My boys were older and had no desire to be in the middle of this heated battle. They chose to move in with grandparents and try to find their own way out of the mess. Our girls were young. The youngest, Hunter Sky, was ten years old, and understood everything was "different," but she didn't completely "get it."

Summer Star, our fifteen-year old, understood very well what was going on. She was heartbroken, angry, and confused. Her goal was to stay strong and be a rock for me. She knew how broken I was and wanted to do everything in her power to fix me.

We spent a few months in Lake Charles, Louisiana, where God put some new friends in our lives who loved and helped us in the beginning stages of our healing. We later moved to Dallas, where we have been since 2005. Once again, God brought beautiful people into our lives who were instrumental in our healing and restoration.

He gave us new friends—friends who took us in while we were still broken. We had nothing to give. We were empty and weak, embarrassed and ashamed. They loved us anyway. They loved as Christ loved. They were the hands and feet of Jesus.

SCARRED

My life would never ever be the same. My children would never be the same. Our marriage would never be the same! Everything is different. I am scarred. You can't see them, but trust me…they're there. I am reminded of them every day.

A minister friend of ours, Dave Roever, served in the Navy during Vietnam and was burned beyond recognition when a grenade exploded in his hand. Dave recently spoke at our church and said, "My scars are clearly visible on the outside. We all have scars, and we will always carry the painful memory of how we got them."

One of the definitions of a scar is "a lasting effect of grief, fear, or other emotion left on a person's character by a traumatic experience."

Scars tell a story. Some people cover them up because of embarrassment. Others don't want to tell the story of how they got them. They feel like they are marked forever in a negative way. We decided to show our scars and tell our story with the hope that it will encourage others to never give up.

"I'LL KNOW YOU'RE BETTER WHEN I SEE YOUR EYES SMILE AGAIN"

My big brother, Dr. John D. McDuff (Johnny), happens to be the most beautiful, Christ-like person I've ever known. He said that my eyes twinkled and danced when I was genuinely happy. Now it was a "pretend happy" that I would try to portray when in public. He told me, "I'll know you're better when I see your eyes smile again." However, I wondered if it were even possible for me to really smile again.

Psalm 13:3 says, *"Turn and answer me, O Lord my God! Restore the sparkle to my eyes, or I will die."* (NLT)

Psalm 39:13 says, *"Spare me so I can smile again before I am gone and exist no more."* (NLT)

"I MISS YOUR SONG"

My father-in-law, Dr. James K. Bridges, was one of the wisest men who ever walked this earth. His wisdom, along with his love, got me through the darkest time of my life. He used to joke with me because I was *always* singing. (There's a slight chance it was annoying at times because, seriously, it was non-stop.) One day he told me he missed my song.

I was the worship leader at our church; I had been singing pretty much my entire life. I always had a song in my heart. My father and his brothers—*The McDuff Brothers*—traveled together and sang for years. I *loved* singing! Get the picture?

Now the desire was gone. I had no song whatsoever! I would read scriptures in Psalms about songs of praise. I started highlighting them and writing beside them in faith that I would sing again. They were baby steps of faith and hope. That's all God expects from us.

Psalm 9:2 says, *"I will be filled with joy because of you. I will sing praises to your name, O most high." (NLT)*

Psalm 13:6 says, *"I will sing to the Lord because he has been so good to me." (NLT)*

Psalm 40:3 says, *"He has given me a new song to sing, a hymn of praise to our God. Many will see what He has done and be astounded." (NLT)*

I still have that same Bible. The binding is taped together, the pages are ripped and stained, but to this day, it's my favorite! It's the one I'm using while writing this book. I love looking back at those highlighted scriptures and the written notes I wrote by faith. I love seeing how God answered my prayers. He restored my hope, my joy, my smile, and my song. He is so faithful! I am so thankful!

Simplified

Yes, I am different! My marriage is different. My children are different. My family is different. My heart is different. My smile is different. My worship is different. My song is different. But it's *better*, way better than it ever was before.

5

(Starla)

TRANSPARENT - Q & A

know this chapter is long, but I didn't want to leave anything out. I had so many questions during my recovery; I needed answers, so I could move on. My prayer is that this helps you on your road to recovery.

The first thing you must do is find a God-fearing counselor ASAP, one that will give you the tools you need to get better. Run, don't walk!

Proverbs 19:20 says, "Get all the advice and instruction you can, so you will be wise the rest of your life." (NLT)

You cannot fix this alone!

Proverbs 12:15 says, "Fools think they need no advice, but the wise listen to others." (NLT)

It takes God, a counselor, you, and your husband—everyone working together. You are in a battle to save your marriage. Get equipped with the wisdom you need to achieve victory.

Proverbs 24:6 says, "So don't go to war without wise guidance; victory depends on having many advisers." (NLT)

Before the Q & A, let me encourage you not to put a timeline on your healing. Everyone's process will be different, as situations are different. Just be willing to give God your heart. Stay in His presence, and do what He wants you to do. Then trust

Him and know that no matter the outcome of your marriage, God will bless you, and He has something better. His ways are higher; His ways are greater, and His ways are always better!

When you go through any experience—marriage, pregnancy, infants, promotion, illness, death of a loved one, whatever it may be—it automatically bonds you with others who have experienced the same thing. You become a member of a "new club." Some clubs are fun and exciting; others are tragedies that you never wanted to experience. Regardless of what it is or how you got there, you are there. You need to gain insight and knowledge from those who have already been there. In order to know the road ahead, ask those who have already traveled it.

I decided a long time ago that I wanted to share my experience to help others, regardless of how uncomfortable it may be.

Because I've walked the road of "life after betrayal," I have ladies asking me the same questions all the time. And because I want this book to help you as a reader, I'm going to be open and honest with you. That's what I needed.

Mother Teresa once said, "Honesty and transparency make you vulnerable. Be honest and transparent anyway."

I had a really hard time finding those who were willing to be transparent. For most, I guess it's just easier to get past it, keep the secret, and not talk about it anymore. I decided a long time ago that I wanted to share my experience to help others, regardless of how uncomfortable it may be. So here goes…

Q. "Why did you stay?" "Should I stay or should I go?"
A. I battled with this one.

After all, I had biblical grounds for divorce—"thou shalt not commit adultery." Helloooo. It's one of the Ten Commandments for cryin' out loud! Nevertheless, I have a few answers for this question.

1. **I had seen women who made hasty decisions to leave a marriage without any attempt to work it out, and their lives were miserable.**

   They never forgave. They were never really happy in their newly attempted relationships. I didn't want to be a bitter, unhappy woman for the rest of my life. I honestly had little hope that we would be restored, but I wanted to be able to say, "I did everything I could to make it work," before I walked away.

   "If you quit you'll never know what might have been." – Gail Lynne Goodwin

2. **I knew deep down inside that everyone has issues, weaknesses, and battles.**

   I now knew what Kendall's were. I knew the warning signs. I knew how to read him. I knew him inside and out. Why in the world would I want to start over with another man who I knew nothing about?

3. **A lady saying goodbye to me from the church we pastored in Houston hugged me tight, got on her knees, placed her hands on my feet, bowed her head, and prayed.**

   I couldn't hear anything she said. But for the next few years, every time I wanted to run away and never look back, God reminded me of that moment and I stayed! I haven't seen her since, so I've never told her how much that prayer affected me. Thank you, Lisa!

   God gave me these scriptures in my quiet times to validate her prayer.

   Proverbs 4:27 says, *"Don't get sidetracked; keep your feet from following evil."* (NLT)

   Psalm 32:8 says, *"The Lord says, 'I will guide you along the best pathway for your life. I will advise you and watch over you.'"* (NLT)

   It wasn't easy. There was one day that I felt very overwhelmed with the weight of everything we were facing. Not only had I lost my marriage, but I'd lost our church, our good name, our income, our home, our vehicles, and everything we had worked to build for twenty-two years. Knowing it was all gone was too much for me.

I got in my car with nothing but a purse and just started driving. I had no plan; I just needed to get away. I wanted to drive as far as the road would take me and never look back. I could hear my phone buzzing the whole time, but I was in such a numb state that I didn't even care.

After a few hours, I pulled over near a park to just sit in the quiet. My mother called me and began to encourage me to go home for my kids. She didn't condemn me. She simply prayed with me and spoke pure love to me. I started the car, and she talked to me the whole ride home.

When I got home, I found out how worried everyone had been. One son was out looking for me and another was waiting in the driveway for me. Seeing the worry in their eyes made me realize how selfish leaving would be. I knew I never wanted to cause my kids any more pain than they were already experiencing.

My mother, my hero, is so full of wisdom. She doesn't say a lot, but when she speaks, it's packed full of solid truth. She has weathered so many difficult storms in her life, but she has never been shaken, she has never wavered from her faith in God. In watching her, I've learned to be still and put my trust completely in God.

Psalm 16:8 says, "I know the Lord is always with me. I will not be shaken, for He is right beside me." (NLT)

Psalm 37:7 says, "Be still in the presence of the Lord, and wait patiently for Him to act..." (NLT)

Psalm 37:5 says, "Commit everything you do to the Lord. Trust Him, and He will help you." (NLT)

I wanted the *best* pathway, so I stayed. I waited, and I trusted.

4. **My husband was different. He was a new man. He was kind.**

His love for me was genuine, deep, and unselfish. He was patient. He let me have my time of grief, unforgiveness, bitterness, and doubt. He stayed transparent. He honored my requests. He set up godly boundaries and loved me when I couldn't love back.

He grew closer and closer to God, putting Him first in everything he said and did. He was a man after God's own heart, and he loved our children differently than he ever had before. They had a new daddy. He was even sweet to my dog. (Kendall is not a dog person, so trust me...this was a big deal.)

He went through counseling and did everything he was told to do. It wasn't easy, but he did it. He died to self. I wouldn't have stayed with the "old" Kendall, but this "new" man made me fall in love with him all over again.

Q. "Did you ever think about 'getting even' with your husband?"
A. Sure I did.

The thought of making my husband feel what I was feeling sounded really good to me. It was crazy how available the opportunities became for me to do just that. Satan had me weak and put traps just about everywhere I went, but I remained faithful! I had enough common sense to know:

1. I didn't want to heap more on top of what I already had to deal with.
2. I didn't want to become *that* woman, and I sure didn't want to hurt another family the way ours was hurting.
3. I didn't want to add more pain and confusion to my children's healing process, but mostly...
4. I didn't want to hurt my Jesus! My heart ached for all the pain that He was feeling.

Proverbs 21:16 says, *"The person who strays from common sense will end up in the company of the dead." (NLT)*

Romans 12:19 says, *"Dear friends, never avenge yourselves. Leave that to God..."* (Paraphrased)

It wasn't my job to "get even" with Kendall or to make him pay. God is the Judge, and He would do what needed to be done. It was my job to trust God, keep my heart and mind pure, and to keep myself from straying into sin.

Q. "How many details do I need to know about the affair?"

A. **A. Everyone is different.**

I've talked with some ladies who didn't want to know anything. They felt like the details would damage them more than the "not knowing."

I was the total opposite. I needed to know everything. I would have questions rage inside of me, and I felt like I would explode if I didn't get the answers. It was the unknowns that drove me crazy.

If you are like I was, then go for it. Ask everything you need to ask. Dig until you've hit bottom. When your questions are all answered, start the climb back up. Then put it behind you and move forward. If your husband refuses to answer, then he has not truly repented. Then take this matter to counseling. He has to get past his pride and secrets before you can heal.

Q. "How do I forgive the other woman?"

A. Well, now here's a doozie!

I was livid! I had no desire to forgive; I wanted to destroy! I didn't want to do anything illegal. I just wanted God to send fire from heaven and do the damage for me. Hey, I'm being honest here. Don't judge. (Drop that rock!)

The chains of unforgiveness were keeping me bound to the attacks of satan on my life, giving him free rein in my thoughts and putting a complete halt to my healing. I was letting unforgiveness eat away at me like a cancer. I realized that I had forgiven my husband but not her. I was living under the same roof with the same man who broke my heart, but I wanted her to burn in hell.

That just didn't make sense to me. I had to take serious steps of faith. I had to release her. I had to let go of my anger. I had to see her as God saw her. I had to love and pray for her.

Matthew 5:44 says, "But I say, Love your enemies! Pray for those who persecute you." (NLT)

If I don't forgive, how can I be forgiven? If I don't show mercy, how can God show me mercy?

Matthew 5:7 says, "God blesses those who are merciful, for they will be shown mercy." (NLT)

By the way, this was not easy, but oh…my…goodness. The reward was incredible! In doing this, I became free. It opened the windows of heaven over my life.

Q. "Was it hard to be intimate with your husband again?"
A. Yes, extremely!

It wasn't special anymore. It wasn't something that only he and I shared as a married couple. Our intimacy had been violated. It wasn't "making love" anymore; it was "sex," and I wasn't interested in "sex."

I wondered if he would be thinking of me or someone else. I wondered if I would ever be able to satisfy him. Would he ever satisfy *me* again? It was hard for me not to picture him with someone else. Every thought that you can imagine ran through my mind. It took a long time, and serious patience from Kendall, to get through this part of our restoration. But we did!

I'm here to tell you that I've never been more satisfied *ever*! It's better now than ever. Kendall loves me very well; he loves me the way God intended. Take that, devil!

God made sex to be a beautiful bond between a husband and wife. He wants us to enjoy sex. When we are faithful to God and to our spouse, sex is beautiful and completely satisfying. It becomes ugly, tainted, and unsatisfying when we get out of God's plan by abusing sex through immoral thoughts, sex before marriage, pornography, and affairs.

There is no bed as comfortable as the one you share with the husband God created just for you. Every other bed leads to destruction.

Q. "Why was my husband unfaithful?"

A. I asked my husband this question so many times, and he couldn't give me a solid answer.

He said it was nothing I did. It was his fault, not mine. He said he never stopped loving me and never wanted to leave me. He never loved her, and he said I met his needs. He said I was a good wife.

Then why? How can a man stray so far from his faith? Why was he willing to risk losing everything—his marriage, children, church, and possessions—for fleeting, meaningless moments of pleasure? How can a man become so blind to sin?

No one is immune to sin, not one of us! We would like to think we are, and sometimes we act as if we are (which in itself is sin), but that's just not the case.

Sin goes back as far as Adam and Eve. How could they disobey God's commands? They lived in paradise and were set up for an eternity of nothing but God's very best. Yet, they threw it all away, and for what? An apple? Seriously? All throughout the Bible there are people—many are our heroes—who had the favor of God on their life, but they still sinned against Him.

1 Corinthians 10:12-13 says, "12 *If you think you are standing strong, be careful, for you, too, may fall into the same sin. 13 But remember that temptations that come into your life are no different from what others experience. And God is faithful. He will keep the temptation from becoming so strong that you can't stand up against it. When you are tempted, He will show you a way out so that you will not give in to it.*" (NLT)

Don't miss the last part of verse 13. God will always show you a way out. Always! Every day all of us will be faced with temptations to sin, and every day we have to equip ourselves with the armor of God in order to withstand the attacks of the enemy. Yes, God will always show us a way out, but if we are not equipped, we won't take it. That's when we fall into the trap of satan.

Q. "Is this my fault? Am I not enough?"

A. No! It is *not* your fault, and you *are* enough!

This haunted me like crazy. I remember how gut-sick I felt every time I would look in the mirror. I would ask myself, "Am I *that* ugly, disgusting, and unattractive? What was so terribly wrong with me that my husband didn't want me anymore? Why was I not enough?" Satan will use this on you every chance he gets to torment you. If you allow him to, it can destroy you.

My husband's sin was not my fault!

James 1:14-15 says, "14 *Temptation comes from the lure of our own evil desires. 15 These evil desires lead to evil actions, and evil actions lead to death." (NLT)*

Proverbs 19:3 says, *"People ruin their lives by their own foolishness..."* (Paraphrased)

People who make excuses are always trying to shift the blame of their sins onto others. I guess it makes them feel less guilty. I know now that it's not anything I did, or didn't do, that caused my husband's failure. It took time, but I also know that I am enough!

Ephesians 2:10 says, *"For we are God's masterpiece. He has created us anew in Christ Jesus, so that we can do the good things He planned for us long ago."* (NLT)

When we feel worthless or even begin to hate ourselves, remember we should have as much respect for ourselves as our Maker does.

Psalm 139:13-14, 17-18 says, "13 *You made all the delicate, inner parts of my body and knit me together in my mother's womb. 14 Thank You for making me so wonderfully complex! Your workmanship is marvelous—and how well I know it. 17 How precious are Your thoughts about me, O God! They are innumerable. 18 I can't even count them; they outnumber the grains of sand!"* (NLT)

God created me exactly the way He wanted me to be—my looks, my talents, my weaknesses, my desires. He created me in His image. I want to live my everyday life pleasing to my Creator. In doing this, I am enough!

Q. "How could God let this happen to me?"
A. Back in my "lamenting phase," I kept asking God why He didn't have my back.
I prayed and prayed against this very thing. I saw it coming, and I warned my husband in plenty of time to avoid it. God was giving him a clear way out, but he wouldn't take it. I didn't understand why God, who had the power to create the universe and all that's in it, couldn't stop my husband from sinning.

Here's the deal: God created man, and He wanted to have fellowship with the man He created. He gave man free will and wanted to be loved by him willingly. Love that's not freely given is not true love. Instead of using that free will to bring God, and Him alone pleasure, we (mankind) used it to bring pleasure to ourselves.

Gods plan was for us to live forever in splendor with Him. God doesn't want us to fail, nor does He want us to hurt. He doesn't want us sick, but we live in a sinful world that is prone to sin and sickness. That's why we need Jesus. That's why Jesus came to earth; He came to make us better.

There was one thought that kept haunting me, the fact that I would never be able to say that I've had a faithful husband. That was lost forever! One night, while having a "fall apart" moment, I went to my closet to have a good cry. I was crying out to God to somehow, with His amazing power, fill that void and pain in me. The fact that my husband wasn't true to me seemed impossible to overcome, but while I was asking God for help, He showed me this: No one, not one person, has been 100% faithful to Him. Our Creator, the Savior of the world, the only One who has ever been faithful, has never experienced true faithfulness from man. Many have desired to be faithful but have failed Him time and time again. Somehow my "impossible situation to overcome" didn't seem so impossible anymore.

My prayer then changed. I began to ask Him to forgive me for the many times throughout my life that I had been unfaithful to Him. I prayed for strength, passion, discipline, and wisdom to live the rest of my life wholly and faithfully committed to Him, His word, and His works. I came out of that prayer time so in love with Jesus and thankful for His faithfulness.

Q. "Do you trust your husband?"

A. Yes, I do.

It feels so good to say that! Do I ever wonder if he will hurt me again? Sure I do. I would be lying if I said no. He's human, and humans aren't perfect. But I refuse to live in fear. I refuse to let satan continually haunt me with that thought. I will live in the beauty of each day, and I will live every day to the fullest. Life is too short to stay in captivity. I have a husband who loves me and shows me every day. So every day I'm going to cherish that love.

The ability to trust didn't come without a fight, though. This was a serious issue that took a lot of work. As I said before, Kendall became transparent. He knew that to win my trust again, he would have to change the way he functioned daily. He'd have to set up boundaries and guidelines. I also set those boundaries in my life to add to that safeguard in our marriage.

The best way to live and walk in freedom is to live a life with nothing to hide. If you have to hide it, you shouldn't be doing it! If you don't want anyone to know, don't do it!

I have such a peace knowing that anyone could look at the history of my computer, read my emails, look at the pictures on my phone, read through my text messages, go through the drawers and closets in my house, look under my bed and in my medicine cabinet. Look wherever you want. I have nothing to hide. (The only thing that would be embarrassing to me is a little dirt here and there and the obvious need to organize.)

Can you say the same? I challenge you to "clean out" your life. Set new godly boundaries for yourself, your marriage, and your children. Live pure, live holy, live free!

Simplified

There are some questions in life that we will never get answered. If we spend our entire lives consumed by the "what ifs" and "whys," we will be miserable and never have peace.

Live with trust, knowing that God works all things together for good.

God didn't answer my prayers the way I wanted Him to. He answered them the way they needed to be answered. He didn't want us to continue our marriage, life, and ministry in the same way. He knew what needed to happen to get us back on course and save our family from further destruction. God's answer was better!

One more thing,

Q. "Was the pain of the process worth it?"
A. YES!

Here's the reward:

- A more beautiful relationship with my Lord and Savior, Jesus Christ. He is my Number One!
- A complete trust and confidence that God is in control.
- He works all things together for His good.
- A marriage that lines up with the word of God.
- A kind of love for my husband that I never even knew existed.
- A knowing that my husband loves me the way God wants him to.
- A family that stayed together, even though the odds were against us.
- A husband, children, and grandchildren that have decided to love God and serve Him in everything they do.

We won! The attack on our marriage failed.

What God has joined together no one can tear apart!

6

(Starla)

DROP THAT ROCK

When reading a book, it's easy to skip over scriptures. I know because I'm guilty of it. Please do not skip this one! This story is life changing, at least it was for me, and it will be for you if you allow it. It gave me the kick in the butt that I so desperately needed.

I was so full of anger and unforgiveness…I didn't like the person I had become.

I was so full of anger and unforgiveness, and I seemed to be getting worse. This is where my stages of grief went too far. It became poison that was eating away at me and slowly destroying me. I didn't like the person I had become. I just couldn't get past the "anger stage." Why should I be stuck with a man without a brain? I saw him as stupid, ungodly, and unable to ever be faithful. I couldn't imagine God ever wanting to use him again in ministry. Why should I suffer the rest of my life because of *his* sin?

I felt "better" than him. I felt like my husband didn't deserve me, and he sure didn't deserve my forgiveness. Then I read these words:

John 8:1-11 says, "1 Jesus returned to the Mount of Olives. 2 But early the next morning He was back again at the Temple. A crowd soon gathered, and He sat down and taught them. 3 As He was speaking, the teachers of religious law and Pharisees brought a woman they had caught in the act of adultery. They put her in front of the crowd. 4 "Teacher," they said to Jesus, "this woman was caught in the very act of adultery. 5 The

Law of Moses says to stone her. What do you say? 6 They were trying to trap Him into saying something they could use against Him, but Jesus stooped down and wrote in the dust with His finger. 7 They kept demanding an answer, so He stood up again and said, "All right, but let those who have never sinned throw the first stones!" 8 Then He stooped down again to write in the dust. 9 When the accusers heard this, they slipped away one by one, beginning with the oldest, until only Jesus was left in the middle of the crowd with the woman. 10 Then Jesus stood up again and said to her, "Where are your accusers? Didn't even one of them condemn you?" 11 "No, Lord" she said. And Jesus said, "Neither do I. Go and sin no more." (NLT)

Verse 7 says, "Let those who have *never* sinned throw the first stone." What? Never sinned? But my sins are little in comparison, right?

I've heard the story many times before, "But I...Felt...Justified." I was throwing stones at Kendall as fast as I could pick them up, seeing myself without sin and wanting my husband to be punished. I had been so focused on making my husband pay for his sin that I didn't even realize that I was sinking further and further into my own pit of destruction.

In that moment, it became so clear to me that I had been playing God. I had appointed myself judge. Kendall was drawing closer to God, as I drifted away. I felt so sick in the pit of my stomach. I dropped that rock so fast and begged God to forgive me.

I felt He was saying to me, "Starla, let Me heal you, let Me take over. I don't condemn you. Now, go and sin no more."

I WAS A SINNER
I needed forgiveness.

1 John 1:8 says, "If we say we have no sin, we are only fooling ourselves and refusing to accept the truth." (NLT)

Romans 3:23 says, "For all have sinned; all fall short of God's glorious standard." (NLT)

All of us are sinners, but check this out. Here's how beautiful our God is...

Romans 3:24 says, "Yet now God in His gracious kindness declares us not guilty. He has done this through Christ Jesus, who has freed us by taking away our sin." (NLT)

Do you see this? We are free! Jesus took away our sins. Now, we need to take hold of that freedom and walk in it! We "humans" have created our own measuring scale of sin. How dare we judge and condemn! Unfortunately, Christians can be the worst. I had become *so* ugly in my condemnation.

I WAS A HYPOCRITE
I was a self-appointed judge.

Matthew 7:1-5 says, "1 "Stop judging others, and you will not be judged. 2 For others will treat you as you treat them. Whatever measure you use in judging others, it will be used to measure how you are judged. 3 And why worry about the speck in your friend's eye when you have a log in your own? 4 How can you think of saying, 'Let me help you get rid of that speck in your eye,' when you can't see past the log in your own eye? 5 Hypocrite! First get rid of the log in your own eye; then perhaps you will see well enough to deal with the speck in your friend's eye." (NLT)

I HAD A HEART OF STONE
I needed a new heart.

Ezekiel 36:26-27 says, "26 And I will give you a new heart with new and right desires, and I will put a new spirit in you. I will take out your stony heart of sin and give you a new, obedient heart. 27 And I will put my Spirit in you so you will obey My laws and do whatever I command." (NLT)

I WAS CONTROLLED BY ANGER
I was giving satan control over my life.

Ephesians 4:26-27, 31-32 says, "26 Don't sin by letting anger gain control over you. Don't let the sun go down while you are still angry. 27 For anger gives a mighty foothold to the devil. 31 Get rid of all bitterness, rage, anger, harsh words, and slander, as well as all types *of malicious behavior. 32 Instead, be kind to each other, tenderhearted, forgiving one another, just as God through Christ has forgiven you." (NLT)*

Richard Paul Evans said, *"We are chained to that which we do not forgive."*

We never look more like Christ than when we forgive.

I REFUSED TO FORGIVE

If I didn't forgive, God wouldn't hear my prayers.

Mark 11:24-25 *says, "24 "Listen to me! You can pray for anything, and if you believe, you will have it. 25 But when you are praying, first forgive anyone you are holding a grudge against, so that your Father in heaven will forgive your sins too." (NLT)*

I had been "praying" and believing but not obeying God's instructions for my own life. Please learn from my mistakes! Don't stay in your season of anger, bitterness, and unforgiveness. Drop whatever rocks you are holding on to. When you forgive, you are free!

I wasn't completely through my healing journey when I experienced this powerful revelation, but this was my pivotal turning point. This is when my eyes were opened and my prayers regained power. This is when my heavy heart started lifting and I began having compassion for my husband instead of condemnation.

Look at these words from Paul on forgiving the sinner:

2 Corinthians 2:6-8 *says, "6 He was punished enough when most of you were united in your judgment against him. 7 Now it is time to forgive him and comfort him. Otherwise he may become so discouraged that he won't be able to recover. 8 Now show him that you still love him." (NLT)*

Kendall had been punished enough. He had done all that he was asked to do. I wanted him to recover; I didn't want him to stay discouraged. It was time to forgive and comfort him. It was time to show him that I still loved him. It was time to repent and heal.

Psalm 32:1-2 says, "1 Oh, what a joy for those whose rebellion is forgiven, whose sin is put out of sight! 2 Yes, what a joy for those whose record the Lord has cleared of sin, whose lives are lived in complete honesty!" (NLT)

"Forgiveness is the key that unlocks the door of resentment and the handcuffs of hatred. It is a power that breaks chains of bitterness and the shackles of selfishness." – Corrie ten Boom

Simplified

Yes, a time of grief is needed to heal, but if you allow it to harden your heart, it turns into sin. Sin is sin in God's eyes. To commit adultery, to lie, to judge, to hate, to live in unforgiveness—it's all sin.

God wants to forgive us; all we have to do is ask, believe in His forgiveness, and then go and sin no more. Trust Him to make you better!

7

(Starla)
OVER MY DEAD BODY

Have you ever said or thought this about any situation? The truth is you never know how you will respond to something until you meet it head on. If you would have asked me before "our storm" if I would stay with my husband if I found out he was cheating on me, I would have boldly without hesitation said, "Over my dead body!" But that's exactly what had to happen. I had to die.

Everyone is selfish. We are born that way. One of the first words we say as a child is, "Mine," and we don't say it sweet. We say it in a mean, ugly tone. No one taught us that; it's instilled inside of us.

Our parents start teaching us to share. Our teachers teach us to think of others. Our coaches teach us to be a team player—there's no "I" in team. Our employers teach us to work together to build a better company. But even though sharing is necessary to function in life, our flesh wants what we want when we want it!

The word selfish is defined as, "lacking consideration for others; concerned chiefly with one's own personal profit or pleasure."

CHARACTERISTICS OF A SELFISH PERSON:

- All about me.
- Always right.
- Go where I want to go.
- Do what I want to do.
- Eat where and what I want to eat.

- Watch what I want to watch.
- Wants to be first.
- Wants adoration.
- "It's my way or the highway."

When you bring "You, Wonderful You" into a marriage, there's going to be conflict. Why? Because you just married another wonderfully selfish human. You both are confident that you know best and will eventually "train" your spouse to see things your way, and that he or she should cheerfully follow you to the ends of the earth. False! False! False!

Marriages fail because of selfishness; you must die to self in order to have a healthy marriage. When we are born again and become a follower of Christ, the old, sinful man dies. We must then put on the new man and live as Christ.

Galatians 2:20 says, "I have been crucified with Christ and I no longer live, but Christ lives in me." (Paraphrased)

THE PROBLEM
We are still humans who do stupid selfish things daily, but why?

Romans 7:15-17 says, "15 I don't understand myself at all, for I really want to do what is right, but I don't do it. Instead, I do the very thing I hate. 16 I know perfectly well that what I am doing is wrong, and my bad conscience shows that I agree that the law is good. 17 But I can't help myself, because it is sin inside me that makes me do these evil things." (NLT)

Becoming a Christian does not immunize you from temptation and sin. Your flesh is willing, but your spirit is weak. There is, and always will be, a war against you. Satan will be relentless in his pursuit to destroy you.

1 Peter 5:8-9 says, "8 Be careful! Watch out for attacks from the devil, your great enemy. He prowls around like a roaring lion, looking for some victim to devour. 9 Take a firm stand against him, and be strong in your faith." (Paraphrased)

We must die daily to our selfish, sinful nature.

Paul says in **1 Corinthians 15:31**, *"For I swear, dear brothers and sisters, I face death daily. This is as certain as my pride in what the Lord Jesus Christ has done in you." (NLT)*

Luke 9:23-24 (NLT) says, *"23 If any of you wants to be My follower, you must put aside your selfish ambition, shoulder your cross daily, and follow Me. 24 If you try to keep your life for yourself, you will lose it. But if you give up your life for Me, you will find true life."*

The word selfless is defined as, "concerned more with the needs and wishes of others than with one's own."

CHARACTERISTIC OF A SELFLESS PERSON:

- Wants others to succeed.
- Puts aside own desires to please others.
- Serves.
- Empowers others.
- Listens, *really* listens.
- Gives without expecting.
- Does good when no one is watching.
- Goes last.

Galatians 5:24 says, *"Those who belong to Christ Jesus have nailed the passions and desires of their sinful nature to His cross and crucified them there." (NLT)*

Galatians 5:13 says, *"For you have been called to live in freedom—not freedom to satisfy your sinful nature, but freedom to serve one another in love." (NLT)*

We have to die to self, die to our sinful nature, and set our minds on things of the Holy Spirit.

Romans 8:5-6 says, "5 Those who are dominated by the sinful nature think about sinful things, but those who are controlled by the Holy Spirit think about things that please the Spirit. 6 If your sinful nature controls your mind, there is death. But if the Holy Spirit controls your mind, there is life and peace." (NLT)

Some of the most beautiful words that my husband spoke to me while on our road to recovery were, "I spent the first twenty-one years of our marriage focused on me. I want to spend the rest of my life focused on you." Swoon...talk about melting.

The most beautiful words I've ever said to my husband were, "I forgive you. I love you, and I trust you".

Simplified
Selfishness = Death.
Selflessness = Life.
Choose life!

Die daily to your sinful, selfish nature. Give the Holy Spirit control of your mind. Kendall and I had to die to self, in order for us to live in freedom and live better.

8

(Starla)
FANS? FRIENDS? FAMILY!

FANS:
WHEN THE POOP HIT THE "FAN"

I've never seen people scatter and disappear so fast. It was messy, and they didn't want any part of it. They didn't want to smell it or get hit by it, and they sure didn't want to clean it up. I've never actually seen poop hit a fan, but can you imagine? You have to admit, it is a pretty funny visual. In my mind, it's an accurate description of what we experienced. You see who your true friends are when your life gets messy. You realize that most of them were just fans.

FANS ARE FICKLE

You know how it is. Teams have a handful of "die hard" fans that are going to be there no matter what. They'll stay season after season regardless of the team's win total. Then there are the "fair weather" fans. They only show support when the team is doing well. They have no real loyalty to the team. They cheer loudly when you're scoring points. But if you fumble, throw an interception, or miss a field goal, they get quiet. At the first sign of serious trouble, they vanish and jump on another team's bandwagon.

"Our team" wasn't winning, so our stadium full of fans left way before the game was over. If only they had stayed, they could have witnessed, firsthand, one of the greatest comeback wins in history—at least for Team Bridges.

In reality, as wrong as it is to be a "fan" that will not plant roots and commit, it's just as shallow to thrive on the cheers of fans and seek the approval of man. We should be living a life to please God and Him alone. We should all be on the same team fighting against the same enemy to achieve the ultimate win.

FRIENDS:
FRIENDS ARE FEW

Walking through pain and brokenness tends to change your reaction to others who are hurting.

We found out fast that "lightweight" friends flee when your life gets ugly. Some leave because they don't want anything to do with your mess. Others go because you don't have anything to offer them anymore. Still others don't know what to say or do, so "fading out" seems like the easy way to go.

That's life. It is what it is. I don't hold grudges; I really don't. It hurt a lot in the beginning, but God has taken care of that pain too. I pray I've learned how to be a better friend, not only when life is pretty, but in the ugly too.

Admittedly, I was guilty of becoming MIA when people had marriage or family drama. I see things differently now. I understand. Walking through pain and brokenness tends to change your reaction to others who are hurting. It's really sad that it takes that for us to love and care for each other the way we are supposed to.

John 13:34-35 says, "34 So now I am giving you a new commandment: Love each other. Just as I have loved you, you should love each other. 35 Your love for one another will prove to the world that you are My disciples." (NLT)

How do we love like Christ? We die to self. We help when it's not convenient, give when it hurts, and turn the other cheek. We love with a sacrificial love. This love not only brings unbelievers to Christ, but it keeps believers strong and united. This love sets us apart.

God gave Kendall and me a few (by few I mean you can count them on one hand) true, genuine friends that walked this entire journey with us. They stayed for the winning "touchdown" in overtime, and they continue to cheer us on today. They have loved like Christ loves, and we are forever grateful. (God sent some incredible new friends along this journey. More on this in "It Took a Village.")

FAMILY:
FAMILY IS FOREVER

Our family is what held us together—siblings who loved no matter what. Blood is thick, and family is strong! We have wonderful, beautiful, strong, and godly parents (on both sides), who loved us, listened to us, counseled us, financially helped us, refused to give up on us, and prayed with us through every step of our healing! I will forever treasure the gift I have in my family. Even though we lost fans and friends along the way, Jesus, our friend (**John 15:15**), never left our side.

Deuteronomy 31:8 says, "Do not be afraid or discouraged, for the Lord is the one who goes before you. He will be with you: He will neither fail you nor forsake you." (NLT)

Ephesians 5:2 says, "Live a life filled with love for others, following the example of Christ, who loved you and gave Himself as a sacrifice to take away your sins." (Paraphrased)

God loved us so much He gave His only son Jesus, and Jesus loved us so much He gave His life for our sins (**John 3:16**). This is the greatest example of love recorded unto man, yet mankind has turned their backs on God as they knowingly live a life of sin. We've turned our backs on His Son by rejecting the gift of eternal life through His sacrifice.

This makes my "offense" seem so small in comparison. It's petty and doesn't even qualify as true rejection. My feelings were hurt. But God, in His love and desire for our well being, sees our pain and desires to heal and restore all that has been stolen from us. God loves us. He not only wants to restore all that we have lost, but even more than we could ever imagine.

Job 42:12 says, "So the Lord blessed Job in the second half of his life even more than in the beginning." (Paraphrased)

Simplified

Yes, we lost fans and friends when our storm hit, but God never left our side! He taught us how to love as He does. He's been faithful to restore all that satan destroyed, but not only that, He made it better!

9

(Starla)
BITTER OR BETTER?

*J**ohn** 16:33 says, "I have told you all this so that you may have peace in Me. Here on earth you will have many trials and sorrows. But take heart, because I have overcome the world." (NLT)*

We all know that in this life we will have many trials and tribulations. That's just how it is. If you've lived more than a decade on this planet, you know this to be true: The question is not, "If," you will experience trials and sorrows; the question is, "What will you look like afterward?" What effect will it have on you?

In late 2009-2010, our family had a solid year of trial after trial, heartache after heartache. Within twelve months, I was diagnosed with breast cancer, my father (John McDuff) had two near-death illnesses, my daughter-in-law (Sara Bridges) was diagnosed with thyroid cancer, my other daughter-in-law (Laura Bridges) had a miscarriage, my father-in-law (James Bridges) was diagnosed with cancer that took his life four days later, my sister-in-law (Kelli McDuff) was diagnosed with cancer that took her life only a few months later.

Every time we turned around, we were getting more bad news. It felt as though our pain would never end. It was too much for a family to have to experience in a lifetime, let alone in one year. It would have been too much to handle alone. I can't imagine having to walk through that year without Jesus.

Isaiah 41:13 says "I am holding you by your right hand—I the Lord your God. And I say to you, do not be afraid, I am here to help you." (NLT)

Through it all, there were many tears and sad days, but God was so very present. We experienced His peace that surpasses all understanding—a peace that only can be experienced through trusting completely that God is in control and that He holds our lives in His hands.

1 Peter 5:10 says, "After you have suffered a little while, He will restore, support and strengthen you, and He will place you on a firm foundation." (Paraphrased)

In the spring of 2011, God brought new life into our family. Our first grandchild, Kanon James Bridges, was born. His birth came in God's perfect timing; it brought our family new life and a new beautiful joy. It didn't remove the sting of disease and death that we had experienced in the previous year, but it did remind us that God loves us and He wants us to experience happiness. He is so faithful!

It's easy to focus on all the bad things that happen to us and to allow the pain of the trials to consume us and control our emotions. Don't let the bad that satan has attacked you with overshadow the abundance of good God has blessed you with.

I've had a lifetime of "bads." Those are easy to remember because they set me back; they consumed me. But I've had way more "goods." God has been incredibly faithful to me and has blessed me so much more than the devil has attacked me.

"Every bitter experience teaches us a better lesson. Every pain builds us higher strengths. Every obstacle leads us to higher ground. The very pain that we felt along our journey is our very best friend. It shall remind us how far we have traveled and how we made it to where we are in the final end." – Ces Peta

Trials can overcome you, if you allow them to, or they can make you an overcomer. You can use them as an excuse to live in misery, or you can use them as an example to others of God's faithfulness.

1 Peter 4:12-13 says, "12 Dear friends, don't be surprised at the fiery trials you are going through, as if something strange were happening to you. 13 Instead, be very glad–because these trials will make you partners with Christ in His suffering, and afterward you will have the wonderful joy of sharing His glory when it is displayed to all the world." (NLT)

What will the world see? What will your outcome be?

- Fearful or Free?
- Miserable or Mighty?
- Defeated or Determined?
- Crushed or Courageous?
- Shattered or Stronger?
- Victimized or Victorious?
- Bitter or Better?

I know how hard it is to stare pain in the eyes and embrace it with open arms. I also know the reward of facing it and letting God fight my battles for me.

Exodus 14:14 *says, "The Lord Himself will fight for us." (Paraphrased)*

Romans 5:3-5 *says, "3 We can rejoice, too, when we run into problems and trials, for we know that they are good for us—they help us endure. 4 And endurance develops strength of character in us, and character strengthens our confident expectation of salvation. 5 And this expectation will not disappoint us. For we know how dearly God loves us, because He has given us the Holy Spirit to fill our hearts with His love." (NLT)*

In my lifetime I've experienced the pain of a crushed heart and broken marriage, the emptiness of depression, the devastation of losing everything, the loss of relationships, the fear of disease, and the sting of death. I have also experienced a God who never fails, the miracle of healing, godly parents who have loved me well, being head over heals in love with my husband, being "Momma" to four beautiful, healthy children, and being "Shoobie" to seven perfect and wonderful grandchildren (and there are more on the way). I really love being Momma and Shoobie.

If given a chance to rewrite some of the chapters in my life, would I? Absolutely!

Would I trade everything I've gained for everything I've lost? Not a chance!

Would I trade everything I've gained for everything I've lost? Not a chance!

I am so thankful that God, in all of His infinite wisdom, has been with me every step along this journey. I can't imagine life without Jesus as my best friend. My life has changed through the years, but my God has never changed! It's because of Him that I smile, laugh, trust, sing, love, and live! It's because of Him that I am better!

James 1:2-4, 12 says, *"2 Dear brothers and sisters, whenever troubles comes your way, let it be an opportunity for joy. 3 For when your faith is tested, your endurance has a chance to grow. 4 So let it grow, for when your endurance is fully developed, you will be strong in character and ready for anything. 12 God blesses the people who patiently endure testing. Afterward they will receive the crown of life that God has promised to those who love Him."* (NLT)

My faith has been tested. I've been attacked left and right. We all have, but God has always proven Himself faithful! To you who are reading this book, regardless of what you've been through, what you're going through, or what storms may come your way, my prayer for you is this:

May you have faith, hope, and trust that God is faithful and that He loves you. God forgives you and will heal and restore you. He will never leave you nor will He ever forsake you. You will overcome!

If you are broken and bitter, please don't stay there. Don't let satan win. If you are healed and better, then rejoice! Tell your story to help others.

Simplified

Yes, many trials will come, but your blessings will outweigh your battles. God wants to fight your battles. Let Him and then trust Him. Refuse to let bitterness win. Determine that those things that have come to destroy you will not make you bitter, but that they will only make you better!

10

(Starla)
MY "JUST RIGHT"

When you first fall in love, you focus on all the wonderful things about that "special someone." Sure there are a few negative things that you easily overlook because you are "smitten" and "twitterpated." They are "the one," the love of your life, and you are ready to spend the rest of your happily ever after with them.

Now, fast-forward a few years down the road to after the newness has worn off. All of those little things have magnified and grown into annoyances you can't see past. In addition, your "perfect match" has changed. A few extra pounds, wear and tear on the bodies. Wrinkles, gray hair, less hair or no hair. They just ain't what they used to be. You are now seeing past the rose-colored glasses of love, and you aren't sure if you like what you see.

Whether it is annoying idiosyncrasies or something as serious as broken vows, your marriage just isn't the same. You've allowed the little things to grow and put a huge wedge between you and your spouse. You start to find yourself comparing. Looking at the "greener grass" on the other side of the fence. (It only looks greener because you aren't close enough to see all of the poop.)

You're unsatisfied. You want what they have. They have a nicer house. He makes more money. He showers her with gifts. He adores her. He's better looking. Their life is so much better than ours. I wish I had their life. The better you make their life look, the worse yours looks. You have entered the danger zone of envy, and God commanded us not to covet.

Exodus 20:17 says, "Do not covet your neighbor's house. Do not covet your neighbor's wife (husband) or anything else your neighbor owns." (Paraphrased)

To covet is to wish to have the possessions of others. It goes beyond admiring and turns to envy. You resent the fact that they have things you don't. You want it. There is nothing innocent about envy.

Galatians 5:19-21 says, "19 When you follow the desires of your sinful nature, your lives will produce these evil results: sexual immorality, impure thoughts, eagerness for lustful pleasure, 20 idolatry, participation in demonic activities, hostility, quarreling, jealousy, outbursts of anger, selfish ambition, division, 21 envy, drunkenness, wild parties, and other kinds of sin. Let me tell you again as I have before, that anyone living that sort of life will not inherit the Kingdom of God." (NLT)

Envy may not be an "obvious" sin, but it is sin. And in God's word, He makes it very clear that if we ignore our sins and refuse to deal with them, we will not inherit His kingdom. Every sin that we act on began as a thought. Every sinful thought is from satan. Change your thoughts, and you'll change your life!

We have to take captive the thoughts in our minds. If we don't, we are giving satan control. Any thought you don't take captive will take you into captivity. You can't take a thought out of your mind no matter how hard you try, but you can replace it with something more powerful. There is nothing more powerful than the word of God. Get in it, meditate on it, and hide it in your heart that you might not sin against Him.

Psalm 119:9, 11 says, "9 How can a young person stay pure? By obeying Your word and following its rules. 11 I have hidden Your word in my heart that I might not sin against You." (NLT)

It's a daily exercise that you must do to equip yourself for the battle against satan. If you have the word of God in you, you have the stronger weapon, and you win!

Philippians 4:8 says, "And now dear brothers and sisters, let me say one more thing as I close this letter. Fix your thoughts on what is true and honorable and right. Think on things that are pure and lovely and admirable. Think about things that are excellent and worthy of praise." (NLT)

There is no love that is as satisfying as the love between a husband and a wife that God has joined together.

Paul is telling us to examine what we put in our minds through television, movies, magazines, books, and conversations. What we put in our minds determines what comes out in our words and actions.

Get your mind and heart in order. Go back to the first love you had with Christ. Get to know and love God's word, and He will restore the first love you had with your spouse. He will make everything that seemed "over" new and more beautiful than before.

Speak positive words over your spouse, and speak life into your marriage. Trust God and let Him restore all that satan tried to destroy. Then watch Him do what He does best—miracles! There is no love that is as satisfying as the love between a husband and a wife that God has joined together.

My God was faithful to restore what seemed broken and beyond repair. Kendall cherishes me. He brings me coffee in bed every morning and kisses and hugs me every time he leaves. He checks in with me throughout the day and cleans up after I cook. (There's nothing more attractive than my man helping me clean.) He satisfies my needs and shows me every day how much he loves me.

The first thing I hear in the morning is, "Good morning, Baby, I love you." And the last thing I hear at night is, "Good night, Baby, I sure love you."

I love Kendall more today than I ever did before. The older we get, the more years we spend together, the more grandbabies we share, the more adventures we have, and the more dreams we see become reality—the more I love him. I love him more and more every day. He is my "just right!"

Simplified

Set your mind on the things of God. Love Him. Love His word, and hide it in your heart. God will not only restore your love and make it better, He will make it the very best that it can be.

Part 2:
Kendall's Chapters 11-21

11

(Kendall)
SCARS

"Never be ashamed of a scar. It simply means you were stronger than whatever tried to hurt you."

– UNKNOWN AUTHOR

Everyone has scars. Some are worn proudly and others are hidden by shame. Every difficult time in our life leaves us with scars. I have been scarred. My family has been scarred. I have scarred others. But do scars have any positive value? Can something good come out of the scars that we have?

Starla and I are drawing back the curtain and allowing you to see the scars in our lives. They're not pretty, but scars have a story to tell. If you will allow me to lay a foundation of scripture that illustrates the value of scars, I think it will help. I believe there is a supernatural potential that exists when we are vulnerable enough to show others our deepest hurts and weakest moments. I think it will help you better understand the reasoning behind this book. So hang on; here we go.

Notice in this passage of Scripture below that Jesus has been crucified and has risen from the dead. Not all of His disciples believed it, so He comes to them and shows them His scars.

John 20:19-20 says, "19 Jesus came and stood among them and said, "Peace be with you!" 20 After He said this, He showed them His hands and side (scars). The disciples were overjoyed when they saw the Lord."

The disciples were having doubts at that moment. What good could possibly come from seeing the scars of Jesus? You see the disciples weren't really sure what had happened. They had been following Jesus for three years, now He was arrested and crucified; His body was now gone, and they are being accused of stealing it. They're wondering, "What has just happened?"

Perhaps you are reading this right now and you are dealing with doubts, disappointment, discouragement, anger, confusion, frustration, questions about the future, and questions about the past. You may be wondering, "What has just happened to my marriage? What has just happened to my husband or wife? What has just happened to me and to my life? What has just happened to everything that I thought I believed in?" If so, you're in good company. The disciples were dealing with all of this and more.

So Jesus showed them His scars, and that's what Starla and I are doing in this book. Our prayer is that you will find supernatural healing, comfort, recovery, and breakthrough in Jesus' name.

Some have scars that they are proud of. Others have scars they're ashamed of. Some have scars that can be seen. Others have scars that no one can see. Scars are not usually considered to be a beauty mark. People often try to hide their scars with clothing or make-up, yet they all have a story to tell.

There are many types of scars—physical, emotional, relational, psychological, social, and spiritual. I have scars that are my fault, and I have others that are someone else's fault. I also have some that are no one's fault. They are simply from an accident. No one is to blame. In any case, I believe every scar has a story to tell.

Here's our story: We experienced a great amount of success in a short time at a young age, while pastoring in Houston. We built the first 2,000-seat Assemblies of God auditorium in Houston. We planted six churches there and pastored in two locations at one time before we were smart enough to use satellite. I was invited to preach District Councils and conferences around the country. I was even invited to preach a Friday night service at the General Council of the Assemblies of God in Washington, D. C., in front of thousands of people.

Then, about twelve years ago, I crashed, burned, and fell. I broke the vows that I made to my wife. I was unfaithful to her, my family, and my God. I hurt the person that I love the most in the world, and I did so in the most selfish and heartless way possible.

I took the most beautiful gift that God has given to married couples and threw it away. I took the delicate heart of my beautiful wife and trampled on it. I thought nothing of the consequences to my precious wife, my four beautiful children, our blessed ministry, or even myself and others. I was reckless, selfish, stupid, arrogant, prideful, and calloused to the consequences of acting out a sin that God so clearly warns against.

I stood before my church with my family at my side. They were there only out of respect for our church, not in support of me. They all wanted to kill me, and rightfully so. I admitted my sin to our church family, asked for their forgiveness in their time, and resigned as pastor. I then submitted myself to the Assemblies of God restoration process. I gave myself to getting right with God, and to winning my wife, my family, and my ministry back.

We started down the road of recovery. It was painful. We were wounded and scarred as a couple. We were wounded and scarred as a family, and I was wounded and scarred as a husband and father. I was scarred, and I had scarred others.

I doubted if Starla would ever forgive me, if my children would ever trust me again, or if I would ever be used in ministry. I felt like such a failure. I was ashamed, embarrassed and broken. I was scarred. The truth is, I didn't feel like I deserved to be forgiven or trusted again. The scars that I saw each time I looked in the mirror continued to be a weight around my neck, pulling me further and further down into despair, discouragement and even depression. The scars were real. The scars were forceful. The scars were devastating. But there are three powerful things that I want to point out about scars.

1. Scars remind us of who we are.

- I have a scar on my arm from a nail on a fence that I fell into in Jr. High School.
- I have a scar on my leg from falling off of a house into a bush, and a freshly cut limb jammed into my leg.
- I have a scar on my neck from surgery.
- I have a scar on my lower leg from a motorcycle accident (which I tried desperately to hide from my parents).
- I have scar on my finger from a knife cut.
- I have scar on another finger from broken glass.
- I have a scar on my toe from my brother throwing a knife into it.

Scars reveal our identity. They remind us of our past. Scars tell the story of our lives and are proof that life has happened. Thomas, the doubting disciple, said, "Unless I see the scars, I will not believe" (**John 20:25**). So Jesus walked up to His disciples and opened His palms to show the scars in His hands. He pulled back His robe and revealed His side that was pierced by the soldier's spear. The scars proved He was alive.

Thomas needed to see the scars in order to believe that Jesus had risen from the dead. He needed to know that it wasn't a terrible joke or a horrible nightmare. The scars were proof that Jesus was alive and had risen from the grave. They had watched Him make an all-you-can-eat fish buffet for five thousand people out of a boy's Long John Silver's fish and chips combo meal. They saw Him turn Perrier into Chardonnay. Yet they still needed convincing.

His scars remind us that Jesus was not just God but also a man. He felt pain and suffering just like you may be experiencing right now. He felt the pain and suffering that you experienced in the past. He certainly knows what kind of pain and suffering you will endure in the future, and He promises to be with you every step of the way.

Our scars may disqualify us from some people's lives, but it qualifies us for others.

I can't tell you how many times Starla and I have had lunch with another couple, only to be asked the question, "Why did you leave Houston and come to Dallas?" (We decided early on that we would be open and honest with people about our past, so that we could walk with integrity and help the people that God would bring into our lives.) That's when we look at each other and show our scars, and the couple often looks at each other and says, "That's why God brought us to you. We've gone through the same thing and are in need of healing."

We also recognize that when we show our scars, it may disqualify us from having a voice in some people's lives. *Our scars may disqualify us from some people's lives, but they qualify us for others.* When you see our scars, you know we have been there and have felt the pain. We have the scars to prove it. We know what you are going through. We know what you are feeling, and we know you can make it.

Jesus' scars remind us of who He is, and our scars remind us of who we are. We are frail, broken, sinful, and fragile humans in need of a Savior.

The second thing about a scar is…

2. Scars remind us of our pain.

In the movie *Jaws*, three men are out at sea searching for the man-eating great white shark. During a lull in their search, they find themselves sharing coffee and horror stories. Each one has scars, and they try to one up each other. One of the characters has scars from a war and another has them from a prior shark attack. The character played by Richard Dreyfus rips open his shirt and points to his chest without speaking a word. One of the others asks, "What? Bypass surgery?" "No," answers Dreyfus, "Betty Sue, seventh grade. She broke my heart."

All of us have scars. You can't live life without being injured in some way. There is not a day that goes by that I am not reminded of my scars. There's not a day that goes by that I don't wish I could turn back time and avoid the steps that caused them. And not a day goes by that I don't regret the scars I've caused others.

Jesus' scars remind us that He suffered and felt pain. Ours also remind us that we have suffered and experienced pain, but I want to share with you some of the wonderful things about scars. Yes, scars remind us of who we are and the pain we've experienced, but the beautiful thing about a scar is…

3. Scars remind us that we can heal.

Scars remind us of the pain and the peril that has come our way, but also of the hope and the healing that followed. Scars tell us that there was an injury but also a victory. Scars remind us that what the enemy meant for harm, God intended for good. Now, let me tell you the rest of the story.

After walking through a process of healing and restoration, we started a church in North Dallas in 2007. And in nine years, God has allowed us to far surpass anything we did in Houston. All of our children are a part of our ministry in Dallas to some degree. Our family is whole and working together to help people find freedom in Jesus Christ.

Yes, I can truthfully say, "God is Restorer, Healer, Provider, and Miracle Worker. He can resurrect that which is dead. He can cause the sun to stand still and the enemy to restore seven times what was stolen. God can roll back the waters for you to walk through on dry ground and can rain the manna down from heaven. He can bring water from a rock, shut the lion's mouth, heal your broken heart, restore your shattered dreams, and bring peace in the midst of your storm. God can and He will." Allow me to show you my scars, and I will show that God can heal.

BEAUTIFUL SCARS
The following story illustrates the beauty of scars:

"Some years ago on a hot summer day in south Florida, a little boy decided to go for a swim in the old swimming hole behind his house. In a hurry to dive into the cool water, he ran out the back door, leaving behind his shoes, socks, and shirt as he went. He flew into the water, not realizing that as he swam toward the middle of the lake, an alligator was swimming toward the shore. His mother in the house, who was looking out the window, saw the two as they got closer and closer together. In utter fear, she ran toward the water, yelling to her son as loudly as she could.

Hearing her voice, the little boy became alarmed and made a U-turn to swim to his mother. It was too late. Just as he reached her, the alligator reached him.

From the dock, the mother grabbed her little boy by the arms just as the alligator grabbed his legs. That began an incredible tug-of-war between the two. The alligator was much stronger than the mother, but the mother was much too determined to let go. A neighbor happened to hear her screams, raced to the scene, took aim, and shot the alligator.

Remarkably, after weeks and weeks in the hospital, the little boy survived. His legs were extremely scarred by the vicious attack of the animal. And, on his arms, were deep scratches where his mother's fingernails dug into his flesh in her effort to hang on to the son she loved. The newspaper reporter, who interviewed the boy after the trauma, asked if he would show him his scars. The boy lifted his pant legs. While looking at his legs, the reporter noticed that the boy had scars on his arms. The boy saw the reporter's eyes and told him, "I have great scars on my arms too. I have them because my mom wouldn't let go."

The real question is, can they see the scars where Jesus wouldn't let go? Some of our wounds are because God has refused to let go. In the midst of our struggles, God has been there holding on to us. Some of the time, when we were running away from God, His grip was growing ever tighter.

I'm so glad that God wouldn't let go of me, and I'm glad he wouldn't let go of you. I'm so glad that as the teeth of sin sunk deep into my soul, God hung on. He hung on so tight that there are scars. Scars that I am proud of. Scars that show others I have been where they are, and God has pulled me through. I have beautiful scars. (Sermon shared by Michael Deaton, August 2003)

The power of the resurrection was strong enough to raise Jesus from the dead, but He is still left with scars. He was able to walk through walls, doors, and overcome all the power of the enemy, yet He is left with scars. Jesus still carries His scars. As He reaches out His hands toward us to receive us as His sons and daughters, He extends nail-scarred hands.

The scars of Jesus are a reminder of the struggle and the fight that He endured for you and me.

But most importantly, the scars are a reminder of His victory over the devil for you and me.

You may be scarred right now. You may be wondering if there is any way to get through this difficult season of your life. I want you to know that God can and will heal and restore you. All you have to do is trust Him. Surrender your hurts, your pain, your failures, and mistakes to Him. He reaches out to you with nail-scarred hands to receive you. He will pick you up and carry you to a better place.

In this book, Starla and I are unpacking our ugly past in order to allow you to see our scars and understand the process God took us through to get to where we are today. It wasn't easy. It wasn't pretty, but now we bear the beautiful scars of God's mercy and grace. Because of these scars, we are better.

12

(Kendall)
DESTROYING HER GIFTS

"Let us always meet each other with a smile, for the smile is the beginning of love."

– MOTHER TERESA

I have always been a very positive person. By personality, I am a sanguine, carefree, and a wing-it junkie. I'm a big-idea dreamer, and I break out in hives just thinking about details. I think you get the picture.

Starla on the other hand is a planner, detailed, and meticulous. She thinks about back-up plans, just in case *Plan A* doesn't work out. She's more melancholy or phlegmatic. Together we make a great team.

The only problem is I didn't recognize, early enough, the gift that Starla is. Instead of seeing our opposite personalities as a perfect match for a complete team, I saw her as a threat to my ideas and plans. I interpreted her planning as only wanting to slow down my momentum and keep me from succeeding. I always wanted to just go for it and get things done. She wanted to plan to ensure that we succeeded.

In reality, there has to be a balance between the two. In order to make sure our plans are successful, she needs me to push her to pull the trigger on certain things, and I need her to help me not to pull the trigger too early.

Starla is also very gifted in discernment. God put her in my life because I really do want to believe the best about everybody, and I will overlook obvious warning signs in people's lives. I misinterpret signs and tell myself what I want to believe about people, even when the signs are saying something different.

Throughout our marriage, I developed resentment toward Starla's role and gifting in our marriage. I didn't value it, and I was wrong. When the time came for Starla to warn me about people in my life who could potentially have a negative effect on me, I ignored her warnings and her discernment. I viewed them as a threat to my personality. I felt like she was just trying to hinder and hold me back.

I silenced her discernment and destroyed her gift by saying things like, "You are just being negative. You just don't see the good in people." All the while, I was pushing away the very gift that God had given me to protect me from my own blind spots. No more! Believe me, if Starla tells me she has a feeling about something or someone, I listen.

Now, I know the fear that some may have about giving that kind of trust and power to someone over your life. You think you'll lose your freedom. You fear that you will be taken advantage of or possibly smothered by someone. But I have found there is freedom and liberty in trusting my wife in the same way she has chosen to trust me as her husband. There has to be equal trust between husband and wife. I now realize that Starla is everything I am not. She is my perfect match, and she completes me.

To the spouse who may be the dreamer, you need the planner in your life. To the spouse who may be the planner, you need a dreamer in your life.

Ephesians 5:21 *says, "Submit to one another out of reverence for Christ."*

We have both found freedom and appreciation for our roles in this marriage, and it has made our marriage *better*. I am so sorry that I didn't recognize Starla's giftings sooner. Our story could have been so much different. I think a lot of our trouble came because I wanted to be in control; I wanted to be in charge. I didn't want anyone telling me what I could or couldn't do. I was fueled by arrogance, near-sightedness, and pride. I felt Starla was a threat to my authority, and because of my stupidity, I hurt the one person God put in my life to protect me from my hardheadedness. God knew what He was doing, but I didn't have a clue. Guys, I sure hope you will learn from my mistakes.

Here's what I learned to do to help me balance the difference of our personalities.

1. **Understand that God places us in the body of Christ as He sees fit.**

   1 Corinthians 12:18 says, "But in fact God has placed the parts in the body, every one of them, just as He wanted them to be."

   In the same way, He puts us in a marriage relationship to help each other.

2. **Verbally recognize each other's value to the marriage.**

   Proverbs 16:24 says, "Kind words are like honey—sweet to the soul and healthy for the body." (NLT)

   Speak positively and confidently to each other about the strengths you bring to the table.

3. **Choose to affirm and encourage the giftings that your spouse has.**

   1 Thessalonians 5:11 says, "Encourage one another and build one another up, just as you are doing." (ESV)

   Use your words in a positive way to encourage each other's unique gifts, and do so on a daily basis.

4. **Don't try to change them to be like you.**

   Romans 15:7 says, "Accept one another, then, just as Christ accepted you, in order to bring praise to God."

   Don't try to change each other; it's a really bad idea. Trust me, God knew what He was doing when He created you and put you together with your spouse.

5. **Believe with all of your heart that God is able to do more through a team that is united and working together, than He can with a team divided and working against each other.**

    1 Corinthians 1:10 says, "I appeal to you, brothers and sisters, in the name of our Lord Jesus Christ, that all of you **agree with one another** in what you say and that there be **no divisions among you,** but that you **be perfectly united in mind and thought.**"

    This takes a lot of effort, but life is so much better when we use our gifts to support each other rather than fight one another.

13

(Kendall)
DON'T BUY THE LIE

"It's funny how humans can wrap their mind around things and fit them into their version of reality."

– RICK RIORDAN, *THE LIGHTNING THIEF*

Too many men in positions of leadership, whether in business or ministry, are constantly told how awesome and amazing they are. I spoke in an earlier chapter of the incredible success we had early in our ministry. I shared that, not to boast, but to show how far I had to fall. I allowed pride and arrogance to rule my life. I thought no one could touch me and that I was above the rule of law. I used to tell people in my church, "If you don't like it here, then don't let the door hit ya where the Good Lord split ya!" I tried to say it in a humorous way, but it came from a very prideful place in my heart.

Once you allow unconfessed sin into your life, it gives place to more sin. Consider the scripture below.

You must learn the lesson because a lesson unlearned will be a lesson repeated.

*1 Corinthians 5:6 says, "Don't you realize that this **sin is like a little yeast that spreads through the whole batch of dough?"** (NLT)*

If not dealt with, the sin you allow into your life will continue to reproduce more and more. My friend, Fred Martinez, told me, "Most men can handle failure, but very few men can handle success." I guess I know which category I was in. Why is that? Because you believe the lie. What is the lie? You are as good as everyone says you are, but you're never *that* good.

You can rebound from failure, if you learn the lesson. *You must learn the lesson because a lesson unlearned will be a lesson repeated.* But if you learn from your failure, you can rebound and succeed again. However, too many men cannot handle success because everyone is kissing up to them, telling them how amazing they are. It doesn't take long to start believing them and buy into the lie.

This is especially true concerning men who are in positions of spiritual leadership, like a pastor. Women will often see you as the second coming of Jesus. You always appear spiritual, prayerful, wise, and compassionate. (We all know better.) Of course, they only see you one hour a week on Sunday morning. Anyone can look good for that long. They don't see you at home, as you get out of bed. Your hair is a mess, your clothes are wrinkled, your breath is horrendous, and you burp on your way to the bathroom (or other noises).

No one but your wife sees you that way. To everyone else you are like Superman. You're exactly what a woman wants in a man. Someone who will be the priest of the home. You are constantly told, "I wish my husband was like you."

First of all, guys, when you hear that the first time, run! Secondly, put that lady in contact with a woman in your church that knows how to "lay hands" on someone. When someone tells you how wonderful you are, it affects you like a drug that creates a feeling you can become addicted to. If you are not careful, you create opportunities for more of those compliments. They seem to silence the fears that are wrestling inside of your head.

The truth is, behind most successful men, there is a person who is afraid of failure. He's afraid to speak of this fear to the person he loves the most, the one whose opinion matters the most to him (his wife). He's afraid to be seen as weak, so he refuses to open up and talk about his innermost concerns. This allows for an emotional divide that only increases with time. It also opens up the door for the enemy to come in and sell you another lie.

As Starla and I began to open up and talk through our hurts, fears, and emotional issues, it didn't drive us apart. It actually brought us closer together, which is the way it should be.

Proverbs 20:5 says, *"The purposes of a person's heart are **deep waters**, but one who has insight draws them out."*

Men and women are totally different. If you ask a guy how his day was, he will say, "Fine," or just explain *what* he did that day. If you ask a woman how her day was, she will tell you how she *feels* about her day. In spite of our differences, we have to find a way to communicate with each other in order to keep the devil out of our marriages. We have to find a way to navigate through the "deep waters" of our emotions.

My failure to keep my vows was never a rejection of Starla. It didn't happen because she didn't watch Monday Night Football with me or meet my needs. Only a coward will use those excuses. I accept 100% total responsibility for the stupid decisions I made that led to my failure as a husband, a father, and as a man.

My failure was because I was deceived to believe that someone other than my wife could make me feel good about myself. I couldn't have been more wrong. My feelings of self-confidence are designed by God to come from "my one and only."

I am not trying minimize or explain away my choices to sin. I will not attempt to pass the blame on to anyone else. I will not attempt to excuse myself from taking total responsibility for my actions. I say these things so you can see how sin has a subtle way of sneaking up on you.

I remember watching a report on how bats would fly into horse stalls at night. They would begin by licking an area around the hoof of the horse to deaden it (like anesthesia). Then they would begin sucking as much blood out of the horse as they wanted. The horse didn't feel a thing.

Sin operates in the same way. It deadens your spiritual consciousness and your spiritual senses. It blinds you to the realities that you are facing. It speaks to your weakness and tells you what you want to hear. Satan is crafty and he is looking for someone to devour.

1 Peter 5:8 says, *"Be alert and of sober mind. Your enemy the devil prowls around like a roaring lion looking for someone to devour."*

Don't let it be you!

Hey husbands and wives, we are on the same team! We are not fighting each other; we're fighting against spiritual forces of this dark world.

Ephesians 6:12 says, *"For our struggle is not against flesh and blood, but against the rulers, against the authorities, against the powers of this dark world and against the spiritual forces of evil in the heavenly realms."*

Our marriages are worth fighting for.

HERE ARE FIVE TAKEAWAYS FROM THIS CHAPTER:

1. **Any sin that you allow in your life will give birth to other sins. So why not stop right now and ask Jesus to forgive you of any sin that you are aware of right now.**

   1 John 1:9 say, *"If we confess our sins, He is faithful and just and will forgive us our sins and purify us from all unrighteousness."*

2. **You can rebound from failure, if you learn the lesson.**
   You must learn the lesson because a lesson unlearned will be a lesson repeated. But if you learn the lessons from your failure, you can rebound and succeed again.

3. **Don't look for praise from anyone other than your "one and only."**

4. **Open up and talk about your deepest fears—but only to your spouse.**

5. **Fight together, not against each other (Ephesians 6:12).**

Better is worth fighting for.

14

(Kendall)
BOUNDARIES

"Boundaries are to protect life, not limit pleasures."

— EDWIN LOUIS COLE

We've all seen the damage that rivers can cause when they overflow and get outside of their banks. The power and surge of the rushing waters will take down trees, homes, buildings, cars, and even human lives. It has no mercy and shows no favor. Outside of its boundaries, it is destructive.

We have all seen the effects of a raging fire that's out of control, moving from one home to the next or from one part of the forest to another. Showing no mercy and taking no prisoners, it leaves behind only the wreckage and ruin of what was once a beautiful home or life-giving forest. The ashes it leaves behind are reminders of its destructive force.

But we all know the great advantage of water and fire when they're used within their proper boundaries. I love to swim in my swimming pool or ski at the lake. What makes it all possible? Boundaries. The water is contained within its boundaries.

There is probably not a smell that I appreciate more than that of a fire. In fact, I have fireside-scented candles in my home and office. Why? Because I love the smell of a campfire. I love camping and cooking over an open fire. There's something amazing about the taste of food cooked over a campfire. I also love the taste of coffee brewed over a campfire. There's nothing quite like it.

What makes this possible? Boundaries. If the fire is contained within its proper boundaries, it has great benefits. However, when it's uncontained and out of control, fire will take what someone took years to build, or nature decades to develop, and reduce it to nothing.

Boundaries are meant to help, assist, and give clarity and purpose. Boundaries are good. They protect and provide for potential to be realized. Boundaries allow you to focus properly and accelerate intentionally. They're established to prevent collision and destruction and to allow for safe travel and smooth transition.

Have you ever seen a car in a high-speed police chase? The car being pursued is breaking the speed limit (a boundary). It crosses from one lane to the next with no regard for others. It crashes into cars on its left and right, as it blazes through traffic. It narrowly misses other cars, but comes close enough to cause them to wreck, collide, or stop and pull over. That was me. I was living life outside of the boundaries Starla and I had established. I broke the boundaries and put myself and others in danger.

You know how it all ends. The car comes to a crashing halt, and that's exactly what happened to me. I came to a crashing halt, leaving my wife, my family, my ministry, others, and myself in the wake of my sin. I caused unnecessary damage in many areas of my life and in the lives of others. The Bible says, "Neither give place to the devil." There is a reason why that scripture admonishes us to live within a certain set of boundaries. Anything else is dangerous and destructive.

Why did God give boundaries, or commandments, to His people (Israel)? Did He want to limit their fun? No. He wanted to maximize their potential and blessings. Unfortunately, many crossed the boundaries and lost their lives in the wilderness.

God gave Adam and Eve boundaries in the Garden of Eden. Satan told them that God did this to limit their potential. He told them that God didn't want them to be like Him, so Adam and Eve believed the lie and crossed the boundaries. They lost their place in the Garden of Eden.

God gave Samson boundaries to live within in order to maintain his anointing and strength. He, too, crossed the boundaries and lost his strength.

So why do people cross boundaries? There is something in every child that causes them to test the boundaries of their parents. There is something in every teen that provokes them to test the boundaries of the system, beliefs, and truth. The same is true of every adult.

Where does all of this come from? According to the verse below, there is a war being waged by the law of sin. Even when you want to do good, evil is right there with you. So how are you rescued from this law of sin? Jesus Christ is the One who rescues you.

Romans 7:21-25 says, "21 So I find this law at work: Although I want to do good, evil is right there with me. 22 For in my inner being I delight in God's law; 23 but I see another law at work in me, waging war against the law of my mind and making me a prisoner of the law of sin at work within me. 24 What a wretched man I am! Who will rescue me from this body that is subject to death? 25 Thanks be to God, who delivers (rescues) me through Jesus Christ our Lord!"

Don't get me wrong! I'm not pulling the Flip Wilson line and blaming this all on the devil by saying, "The devil made me do it." I take full responsibility for my actions. I have to. God has given each of us the power to trample over all of the enemy and his power.

Luke 10:19 says, "I have given you authority...to overcome all the power of the enemy."

We just have to be willing to use that power and not be deceived by the enemy. Learn to live within healthy boundaries.

HERE IS WHAT I LEARNED TO HELP ME ESTABLISH HEALTHY BOUNDARIES.

1. **You have to set clear boundaries based on your weaknesses and your personality.**
   Different people will need different boundaries. Base them on your personality, weaknesses, and tendency to do certain things. Boundaries should be customized to the person and to the couple.

2. **You have to be held accountable to live within those boundaries.**
   It is important that you are accountable to your spouse, and possibly to another friend or advisor, who can look you in the eye and ask you, "How are you doing?"

3. **You have to continually be reminded of those boundaries.**

This may be an exercise that you do with your spouse or one you do each morning in your private time with the Lord. Remind yourself of certain boundaries in order to keep it fresh in your mind. This allows you to be prepared when the enemy tries to tempt you to cross that line. If you remind yourself each morning, you have already prepared yourself for any temptation that may come. You've already determined that you would be faithful to your spouse and to your agreed boundaries.

I have a friend who prays every morning before he leaves his home, "Lord let me come home faithful to my wife today." He reminds himself of his boundaries on a daily basis.

- Let me say to the person who has already crossed the boundaries: You are living with the consequences of that decision, and you probably understand the importance of these three steps. So don't delay. Act on it now. Have a discussion with your spouse about new healthy boundaries for you both.
- To the one who has crossed the boundaries and hasn't been caught yet: Remember God's word.

*Numbers **32:23*** *says, "Be sure your sin will find you out." (KJV)*

- To the one who has never established boundaries but realizes you're playing with fire: Remember, if you play with fire, you will get burned.

Set new boundaries that will help your life be better. Below is a set of boundaries Rick Warren has provided for his church staff.

10 COMMANDMENTS TO HELP CHURCH STAFF MAINTAIN MORAL INTEGRITY

As Christian leaders, we need to be above reproach.

*In **1 Corinthians 10:12**, Paul wrote, "Don't be so naive and self-confident. You're not exempt. You could fall flat on your face as easily as anyone else. Forget about self-confidence; it's useless. Cultivate God-confidence." (MSG)*

That's why I established these Saddleback Staff Standards for maintaining moral integrity:

1. Thou shalt not go to lunch alone with the opposite sex. *
2. Thou shalt not have the opposite sex pick you up or drive you places when it is just the two of you. *
3. Thou shalt not kiss any attender of the opposite sex or show affection that could be questioned. *
4. Thou shalt not visit the opposite sex alone at home.
5. Thou shalt not counsel the opposite sex alone at the office, and thou shalt not counsel the opposite sex more than once without that person's mate. Refer them.
6. Thou shalt not discuss detailed sexual problems with the opposite sex in counseling. Refer them.
7. Thou shalt not discuss your marriage problems with an attender of the opposite sex.
8. Thou shalt be careful in answering emails, instant messages, chat rooms, cards, or letters from the opposite sex.
9. Thou shalt make your secretary your protective ally.
10. Thou shalt pray for the integrity of other staff members.

* The first 3 do not apply to unmarried staff.

Ephesians 5:3 says, "But among you there must not be even a hint of sexual immorality, or of any kind of impurity, or of greed, because these are improper for God's holy people."

(http://pastors.com/maintaining-moral-purity-in-ministry/)

I think these are spot on. We've adopted them for our own church and ministry.

15

(Kendall)
WARNING SIGNS!

"Nobody ever listens to me."

– YELLOW TRAFFIC LIGHT

The Grand Canyon is one of the most beautiful sites to behold in the entire world. I had the privilege of hiking it with my father and my brothers when I was a teenager. What a memory! I'll never forget, as we reached the bottom of the vast canyon, we wiped the sweat from our brows and sat on rocks in the Colorado River. My father pulled a pocket New Testament from his jacket pocket and read from **Hebrews 11:3**, "By faith we understand that the universe was formed at God's command, so that what is seen was not made out of what was visible." He told us to look around and realize that the majesty of what we were beholding was made by the hand of God—from the invisible world of His supernatural Kingdom.

It made such a lasting impression on me that I vowed to do the same thing with my sons when they were old enough. Well, sure enough, I did just that. When my two sons were teenagers, we made the same journey to the Grand Canyon. We arrived and stopped by the information center to ensure that the proper trails were open. The lady behind the desk asked when we were planning on hiking the canyon. I said, "First thing in the morning." She followed with another question, "Are you spending the night at the bottom?" I said, "No ma'am, we are hiking down and out the same day."

She had a very concerned look on her face. "I would strongly advise against it," she told us. I assured her that we would be fine; I had done it before. I sounded so confident.

She again advised, "We have to helicopter people out of the canyon every summer who become over-exhausted, dehydrated, or just too weary to make it out. The cost is very expensive. She then called for a park ranger and told on us like a tattletale on the playground at school. The park ranger then advised against us doing it as well.

I have to tell you, my sons and I were so determined to hike the canyon in one day that nothing was going to stop us. So early the next morning, we set out toward the bottom of the Grand Canyon. Once we reached the bottom, we sat on the same rocks in the Colorado River, and I read the same scripture from **Hebrews 11:3**. I read from a Palm Pilot (if anyone remembers what those were).

As we began our journey toward the top, we passed another park ranger. He asked us, "What are you doing?" We said, "We are hiking out of the canyon." He looked at his watch. "You shouldn't try it at this time of the day. Besides, the next water station is broken and there is no water for several miles. I would advise against you doing this," he lectured.

We respectfully thanked him for his advice, but we were committed at this point. We had no camping gear to spend the night at the bottom. We made our journey to the top without much difficulty.

I tell you this story because it has since occurred to me that this is the way temptation works in our lives. First, you get an idea in your mind. Next, you make a decision to pursue it. You still have an opportunity to turn back, but the further down the road you get, the more committed you are. Then, you finally reach the point of no return. There was a time when you could have turned back without much difficulty. But the more you think and talk about it, and the more you ignore the warning signs, the more difficult it becomes to do the right thing.

When does a person reach the place where they can't turn back? I'm sure it is different for each person, but it starts with a thought. Then there are a series of warning signs and roadblocks that are walked past in order to make the wrong decision. Perhaps you told yourself that you could turn back at any time, but you were deceiving yourself. The Bible tells us to not give the devil an opportunity to lead us into sin.

Ephesians 4:27 says, "And do not give the devil an opportunity to lead you into sin." (AMP)

I am convinced that God put many warning signs in front of me that I ignored in order to follow through with my sin of unfaithfulness. I recognize my failure was not the result of an immediate breakdown in judgment or poor decision-making. It was a process that took place over time. I overlooked all of the cautionary signals and finally crossed the line into moral failure. God put many warning signs in my pathway to keep me from failure, but I looked past them.

10 WARNING SIGNS I IGNORED

1. **God's Word**

   Psalm 119:9-11 says, *"9 How can a young person stay on the path of purity? By living according to Your word. 10 I seek You with all my heart; do not let me stray from Your commands. 11 I have hidden Your word in my heart that I might not sin against You."*

   There were many times that the Word of God was clearly speaking to me. But it is possible for us to ignore what is intended for us and only listen to what we want to hear.

2. **The Holy Spirit**

   Psalm 106:33 says, *"For they rebelled against the Spirit of God."*

   I recognize now that there were many times the Holy Spirit would wrestle with me and speak and call to me. Yet, in my rebellion, I ignored the warning signs of the Holy Spirit. Oh, how I wish I would have listened!

3. **My wife's discernment**

   1 Corinthians 12:7-8 says, *"7 But the manifestation of the Spirit is given to each one for the profit **of all**: 8 for to one is given the word of wisdom through the Spirit... to another discerning of spirits." (NKJV)*

Many times through the years, my wife would have a discerning spirit about an individual. I often ignored it and labeled it as a negative attitude. She was right.

4. My conscience

Acts 24:16 says, *"So I strive always to keep my conscience clear before God and man."*

There were more times than I can recount that my conscience cried out. However, over a period of time, one can become calloused to the cry. You begin to justify your actions with stupid reasoning—not enough reasoning to make sense, but just enough to quiet the cry of the conscience.

5. Friends

Proverbs 27:6 says, *"Wounds from a friend can be trusted."*

Several times, individuals whom I had allowed to have a place of accountability in my life came to me and warned me of something they were discerning. I began to ignore and drown out their warnings with lies to myself. I believed I was smarter than they were. I thought I could fool them. I was so full of pride that I wanted to make them think they were wrong, rather than admit they were right. How foolish.

6. Apparent consequences

Proverbs 28:13 says, *"Whoever conceals their sins does not prosper, but the one who confesses and renounces them finds mercy."*

So many times I would think of the consequences of my actions, but I was blinded by my own arrogance. I thought I could get away with it and no one would ever know. Jeopardizing my marriage, family, children, ministry, and my family's ministries were all apparent consequences. I was aware of them, yet I continued down a path of destruction. I believed that I could turn back at any time and still be all right.

Somehow during the process, I began to doubt, to some degree, that I would reap the consequences of my actions. I really began to think that God would forgive me at any point and overlook my past, and I wouldn't be held accountable. I had a distorted view of God's grace. I realize now that His grace does not nullify His judgment, nor does it prevent Him from disciplining His children for their disobedience. Because He loves us, He will chasten and rebuke us if we need it.

7. Letting down my friends

Romans 14:12 says, "So then, each of us will give an account of ourselves to God."

I knew that if I were to fail, I would let down my friends and colleagues, yet I ignored that warning sign. I knew I would be held accountable for that, yet I walked right past the warning signal.

8. Non-Christians who will never come to Christ

Matthew 5:16 says, "In the same way, let your light shine before others, that they may see your good deeds and glorify your Father in heaven."

I recognize now, more than ever, that there are individuals who will never come to Christ because of my failure. I didn't handle the light God had given me properly. That's not an easy burden to carry. I knew it full well, yet I ignored this truth anyway.

9. Christians who will fall away

Psalm 78:41 says, "Yea, they turned back and tempted God, and limited the Holy One of Israel." (KJV)

I know some will fall away from following Christ because of my actions. My prayer is that they will look to Jesus and not to man, but I am fully aware I have scarred many individuals who may miss eternity due to my actions. This is not easy to deal with.

10. Examples of others who have fallen

1 Corinthians 10:12 says, "So, if you think you are standing firm, be careful that you don't fall!"

You would think that after seeing so many go down the road of self-destruction, it would be enough to warn me of the snares of the enemy. Somehow, I believed the lie that I could get through this, get out of it, and not get caught. So stupid!

These are a few of the warning signs that I believe God allowed to speak to me. The Bible promises: "No temptation has overtaken you except what is common to man. And God is faithful; He will not let you be tempted beyond what you can bear. But when you are tempted, He will also provide a way out so that you can endure it." (**1 Corinthians 10:13**) I had the way out. I just didn't take it. My prayer is that you will learn from my mistakes and pay attention to the warning signs.

16

(Kendall)
WILL THIS ALWAYS BE THROWN IN MY FACE?

"Broken trust and anger will close a heart until honesty and love is once again found."

— UNKNOWN AUTHOR

I have sat with guys who have come to me for advice on how to get through an affair or a confession of infidelity. They have always confessed that one of the biggest fears of trying to work things out is, "Will my wife always throw this in my face?"

I had one minister tell me, "I would rather divorce, start over, lose all my friends, and take a chance on what this will do to my kids, than live with this being held over my head every day for the rest of my life." I understand that fear. I guess that is always a possibility, but if my wife was going to take a chance on me again and trust me to be faithful to her, then I was going to have to trust her as well. Was there a fear that this would always be thrown in my face? Yes.

In fact, I can still remember one day when we were sitting on my office floor. I committed to Starla that I would spend the rest of our marriage making this up to her. She looked at me and said, "You may not like the person I become when we get through this." I remember thinking, "Oh my, what am I in for?" But I knew the right thing to do was to work my tail off trying to fix what I had broken and heal what I had hurt.

I can tell you this, Starla did take a while to process and find her healing. The fact that we are writing this book is a testimony to the healing process, but it took a while. There is no magic formula on how long someone takes to heal. Some heal quicker than others. Starla was a slow healer. I learned that the deeper the love, the deeper the hurt. She had loved deeply and was hurt deeply.

There were times when I thought we were past certain things, only to find out that I was mistaken. Did that ever frustrate me? Sure it did, but I always reminded myself that I was the one who created the hurt. It was my job to find a way to allow healing. God was faithful to help me, and He brought healing.

I sat across the table from a man who shared with me that he had been unfaithful to his wife. One of his concerns was relinquishing his authority in order to be restored. He didn't want to have to give access to his cell phone or email and always give an account of where he was at all times. He said, "I don't want to always feel like a prisoner."

I know it sounds like he was still trying to hide things, and he may have been, but there was a different concern that is real. No matter what *his* truth is, his fear of never getting control back once completely giving it up is real. (Believe me this is bigger than the TV remote control.) Again, I know what some of you are thinking right now. You're thinking, "It doesn't matter what he feels or thinks. He messed up, and he should do whatever it takes to make this right." Yes, that's exactly what he should do, but too many individuals miss out on the beauty of a restored marriage because of the fear of something that may never happen. Yes, he had been busted, and he'd admitted it. He was truly sorry for what he had done, but he couldn't get past the feeling that if he surrendered his authority, rights, and privileges, he might never get them back again.

He and his wife's restoration were being hindered because he was unwilling to be accountable and transparent with her. Regardless of whether or not you remain faithful, the healing process requires submitting to one another.

Ephesians 5:21 says, "Submit to one another out of reverence for Christ."

I know the fear of never getting back the reins of your household. I know the fear of never being the priest of your home again. I know the fear of losing your voice in the marriage and with your children. I battled with all of those concerns. However, these are the very reasons why many walk out of marriages and refuse to walk through the restoration process.

Now, listen to me carefully. If the process is done right and is completed, there will be restoration. Restoration in itself means that things are placed back in their right order.

Behavior that is monitored is behavior that is modified.

Additionally, there is absolutely no reason why any husband or wife should ever care if their spouse has access to their private life. The truth is the accountability is good for you. Accountability probably would have kept me from making the poor choices that I did. It's good for everyone. There is a reason why people act differently when they are around others. *Behavior that is monitored is behavior that is modified.*

Remember, if your spouse is going to trust you to be faithful after failure, you will have to trust her to restore rightful authority in due time. Believe me, it will come. Starla has been amazing. She is a new woman, and I'm a new man. We are happier now than we have ever been. I am more in love with Starla today than I ever was before. The fact that we are sharing our story is a testimony that God has restored us. If He can do it for us, He can do it for you.

HERE IS WHAT WE DID TO HELP ONE ANOTHER HEAL.

1. **Know yourself.**
   Every one heals differently. Don't try to put yourself on someone else's timeline. Some have other issues from the past that are just now resurfacing and having to be dealt with. Know yourself and trust your heart for the timeline.

2. **Be Yourself.**
   Allow yourself to feel what you are feeling. Some people will try to tell you how you should think, act, or feel. They are not you. Be yourself. Be bold and courageous enough to recognize the feelings you have and deal with them accordingly.

3. **Allow yourself to love and be loved.**
   God made us to love and to be loved. I know there is a tendency to want to shut down and never love again, or to shut down and never allow yourself to be loved again. This would be a mistake. Allow yourself the opportunity to be loved and take the risk of loving again.

4. **Control your thoughts.**
   Thoughts are a powerful force. With our thoughts we set a pattern for success or failure, for healing or hurt.

The Bible tells us in **2 Corinthians 10:5**, "We demolish arguments and every pretension that sets itself up against the knowledge of God, and we take captive every thought to make it obedient to Christ."

When the thoughts of doubt, fear, and overwhelming anxiety try to take control of you, flip the script and turn the tables on the enemy. Take those thoughts captive and make them obedient to Christ.

5. **Leave the past in the past.**
   I know this sounds easier than it really is.

The Bible tells us in **Philippians 3:13**, "But one thing I do: **Forgetting what is behind** and straining toward what is ahead..."

So I know that it is possible. There is great value in leaving the past in the past. This is in no way saying that the past should not be dealt with. Obviously, you can't ignore what has brought you to this point in your life. But once the problem is identified and steps have been taken to deal with it, leave it in the past.

This will definitely make things better.

17

(Kendall)
CONTEMPLATING SUICIDE

"The Sun will rise again!"

If you have never felt the feeling of hopelessness, then you probably won't get what I am about to say. But if you have ever felt the feeling of being without hope, then you will get it. It is like being smothered, not able to find your breath. It's as if the night has fallen and the sun refuses to shine again.

The weight of despair, anxiety, and overwhelming sense of abandonment looms over your soul. It's as if you are attempting to look up, but you see no possible way out of the present situation. The fear of never being whole again completely engulfs you. You try so desperately to find something to believe in or something to give you hope, but there is nothing. The darkness is more than you can bear.

Let me say before I go any further that I am an extremely positive person. I see the glass half full and the good in nearly everything. My blood type is B+ for crying out loud! I struggle with sharing this part of the story. But I want to help people, so I am being as vulnerable as I possibly can.

The day I confessed to Starla, the spirit of suicide came over me. It was like a dark heavy cloud that just came in and surrounded me. I saw no other way out. All of my failures were lying in front of me. The shame and embarrassment of hurting my wife, children, family, and friends was more than I could bear. I sobbed and sobbed. I was broken and humiliated. I had done the very thing that I promised I would never do.

How could I have been so foolish? I had seen so many other people make this same mistake, commit this same sin. I had seen the way it had torn families apart. Marriages were ruined. Children were riddled with doubt and uncertainty. I couldn't bear the thought of facing anyone. I truly believed that Starla would be better off dealing with my death than having to deal with forgiveness and my failure.

I believed that my children would be better off dealing with my death rather than having to face their father who had failed them as well. As I look back on it now, I realize all of the wonderful moments I would have missed with my family. I would have missed weddings and the births of grandchildren. I would have missed seeing them all grow up into men and women of God. Each one of them is amazing!

I'm sorry I drug my family through all of this, and I am so sorry that I was not the husband I should have been. I was not the protector of my home, nor was I the protector of my children. I always wanted to be a hero to my kids. I broke their hearts and shattered their dreams. I caused them more unnecessary embarrassment and heartache than any child should ever have to deal with. Along with all of that, I am so sorry that I almost took away the possibility to give God a chance to heal us all.

Suicide seemed to make sense to me at that moment. The truth was that the contemplation of taking my life was just as selfish as the sin I had committed. I wasn't really as concerned about my family as I was about my shame. Again, it was all about me. But in that moment, the devil tried to deceive me into making it about others and not myself. Satan is a master deceiver.

Revelation 12:9 says "...satan, the one deceiving the whole world—was thrown down to the earth with all his angels." *(NLT)*

John 8:44 says, "the devil...when he lies, he speaks his native language, for he is a liar and the father of lies."

I've never before, or since, felt that spirit of suicide come over me. I know what it was like in that moment to literally fight for my life, to grasp for the next breath. I know the only thing that pulled me through that difficult struggle were people who were praying for me. (I think some were praying for me to stay alive so they could kick my butt for themselves.)

Regardless of their motivation, prayers bombarded heaven, and it was as if the cloud began to lift. I could breathe again. Like the prodigal son, I finally *came to my senses* and came home (**Luke 15:17**).

Don't get me wrong. There was no celebration when I went home. It was like walking into a funeral. You know that feeling when you walk in and you see people you haven't seen in a while, and you want to express happiness for seeing them, but you have to maintain your composure because of the reason you're really there. There had been a death alright—the death of our marriage. It was the death of vows I had made; it was the death of an unbroken love. I walked in, and it was painfully awkward to say the least.

Even so, I was going to try my best to make it right, regardless of how painful it might be. And believe me, it was painful and difficult. Facing my family, wife, sons, daughters, and parents was the most humiliating moment of my life. My youngest daughter Hunter (ten years old at the time), looked me in the eyes and said, "But Daddy you promised you would never do this!" My heart was ripped out all over again.

The days that passed seemed to fall from the sky in slow motion. I wondered if they were ever going to hit the ground. It's as if they would never end.

I remember waking up one morning before dawn and walking outside to read my Bible and pray. I waited long enough to see the sun rise. It wasn't much different than any other day. There wasn't anything spectacular about this particular sunrise, but I heard a voice speak to me in my spirit that day. I heard the voice say, "The sun will rise again."

As sure as the sun will rise again (and it did), the darkness will lift, and the sun will rise on this dark night of your life.

I contemplated what that meant for me that day. I was asking God to show me how all of this was going to work out for good. I was willing to put whatever effort was necessary into rebuilding our marriage, but I wondered if Starla was going to be able to do the same. I wondered if she was ever going to be able to forgive me or trust me again, or would it just be best for us to go our separate ways? That's when I heard it again: "The sun will rise again."

I asked the Lord, "What are you trying to say to me today?" Here's what He said, "As sure as the sun will rise again (and it did), the darkness will lift, and the sun will rise on this dark night of your life." That's all I needed.

Every day since then, when the sun comes up in the morning, it's a promise to me that God's plan of restoring a marriage is bigger and better than the devil's plan to destroy it. Here is what I want to say to you today:

If you are wondering if it's worth the fight to rebuild a marriage, I would say, "Yes it is."

If you are struggling with the thought of suicide, I speak to that spirit to come off of you now, and I declare that the cloud and heaviness of suicide lift from you, in the name of Jesus. You are God's child. His Spirit is in you. He created you to live an abundant life according to **John 10:10**. Be free, in Jesus' name.

If you are wondering if it is going to get better, yes it will. Maybe you've made some mistakes, but God's grace is all you need (**2 Corinthians 12:9**). The sun will rise on this dark night in your life, and let the sun be a promise to you as well.

Remember this lesson from the children of Israel. As they were facing the Red Sea, Pharaoh's army was approaching them from behind. The Red Sea was in front of them, and there was nowhere for them to go. They were completely hemmed in—hopeless. They had no escape hatch. In these moments, people panic, give up, and listen to the voice of the enemy. Then the spirit of hopelessness suffocates them.

I want you to always remember this truth: During the darkest times of your life, God is still in control and is working to make your life better.

Notice what God did when Israel was facing this impossible situation.

***Exodus 14:21** says, "Then Moses stretched out his hand over the sea, and all that night the Lord drove the sea back with a strong east wind and turned it into dry land. The waters were divided (or parted)."*

Here is a thought that will change your life: God works the night shift. All that night, God was driving back the waters. Yes, it may seem like there is no hope, but it always gets the darkest just before dawn.

When the children of Israel closed their eyes that night, there was a Red Sea in front of them. When they opened their eyes in the morning, there was an eight-lane highway. God is going to make a way for you!

Even though it may seem dark in your life right now, and you can't see your way through this, God has not forgotten you. He has not abandoned you. He is actually working for you right now. The sun will rise on this dark night in your life, and God will allow you to see that He has made a way for you.

Have you ever been trapped underneath a heavy object? You need someone to come along and lift the load so you can be free. It's the same spiritually. Let someone share this struggle with you.

HERE IS WHAT I DID TO "HANG ON" WHEN EVERYTHING IS "GOING WRONG."

1. **Trust the faith and prayers of someone else until the heaviness lifts.**

   There are some things you just can't do on your own. You need to trust others to help carry your load. Remember the paralyzed man in Mark 2 that had four friends who brought him to Jesus? They couldn't get in through the crowd, so they climbed on the roof and tore a hole in it. Then they lowered him to Jesus, and he was healed.

   Mark 2:3-5 says, "3 Some men came, bringing to Him a paralyzed man, carried by four of them. 4 Since they could not get him to Jesus because of the crowd, they made an opening in the roof above Jesus by digging through it and then lowered the mat the man was lying on. 5 When Jesus saw their faith, He said to the paralyzed man, 'Son, your sins are forgiven.'"

2. **Don't give up.**

   Galatians 6:9 says, "Let us not become weary in doing good, for at the proper time we will reap a harvest if we do not give up."

   I know there will be times that you feel like giving up. There will be times that you feel like you can't go on. There will be times that you think it is best to quit. Don't give up. There is a "proper time" for you.

3. **Let the sun be your promise.**

   Every morning when you see the sun come up, tell yourself that the sun will rise on this dark night in your life. The more you see it, the more you say it, and the more you will believe it.

The new day will be better. The sun is your promise. As the sun rises today, take a moment and stand in the sun. Turn your face toward the sun and notice that your shadows fall behind you.

18

(Kendall)
CONSEQUENCES

"You are free to make whatever choice you want, but you are not free from the consequences of that choice."

– UNKNOWN AUTHOR

Why did I not consider the consequences of sin? Why did I think I could get away with it? Did I really hope God would not hold me accountable for my sin? Was I really that deceived? Are we really that deceived? Yes, I believe we are.

When someone commits a sin and there seems to be no immediate consequences, it makes it easier to do it again.

Sin is a deceiving force. When someone commits a sin and there seems to be no immediate consequences, it makes it easier to do it again. I know that's the way I was. I never intended to be unfaithful to my wife, nor did I plan on hurting my family or damaging others. You may ask, "What was I thinking?" I wasn't. That's the problem.

This following story comes from Alan Smith's, "Thought for the Day," and it illustrates how deceptive and destructive sin can be.

The following incident won the runner-up prize in the 1999 Darwin Awards:

A Vermont native, Ronald Demuth, found himself in a difficult position. While touring the Eagle's Rock African Safari (Zoo) with a group of thespians from St. Petersburg, Russia, Mr. Demuth went overboard to show them one of America's many marvels. He demonstrated the effectiveness of "Crazy Glue"... the hard way.

Apparently, Mr. Demuth wanted to demonstrate just how good the adhesive was, so he put about 3 ounces of the adhesive in the palms of his hands, and jokingly placed them on the buttocks of a passing rhino. The rhino, a resident of the zoo for the past thirteen years, was not initially startled as it has been part of the petting exhibit since its arrival as a baby.

However, once it became aware of its being involuntarily stuck to Mr. Demuth, it began to panic and ran around the petting area wildly making Mr. Demuth an unintended passenger.

"Sally [the rhino] hasn't been feeling well lately. She had been very constipated. We had just given her a laxative and some depressants to relax her bowels, when Mr. Demuth played his juvenile prank," said James Douglass, caretaker. During Sally's tirade two fences were destroyed, a shed wall was gored, and a number of small animals escaped. Also, during the stampede, three pygmy goats and one duck were stomped to death.

As for Demuth, it took a team of medics and zoo caretakers to remove his hands from her buttocks. First, the animal had to be captured and calmed down. However, during this process the laxatives began to take hold and Mr. Demuth was repeatedly showered with over 30 gallons of rhino diarrhea. "It was tricky. We had to calm her down, while at the same time shield our faces from being pelted with rhino dung. I guess you could say that Mr. Demuth was into it up to his neck. Once she was under control, we had three people with shovels working to keep an air passage open for Mr. Demuth. We were able to tranquilize her and apply a solvent to remove his hands from her rear," said Douglass. "I don't think he'll be playing with Crazy Glue for a while."

What in the world was Mr. Demuth thinking???? I believe it is safe to say that he wasn't thinking at all! I don't want to be too harsh and critical, though. I have to remember all the times in my life when I have "attached" myself to something sinful. The results were just as disastrous, and I have often found myself wondering, "What was I thinking?" The truth is, I really wasn't thinking at all.

That's the very nature of sin. We "attach" ourselves, thinking we can always quit whenever we want to. We don't even consider what the consequences will be. Perhaps we need to be reminded every now and then of just how disgusting the results of sin can be.

James 1:14-15 says, *"But each one is tempted when he is drawn away by his own desires and enticed. Then, when desire has conceived, it gives birth to sin; and sin, when it is full-grown, brings forth death." (NKJV)*

To what (or whom) have you attached yourself?

I think this story clearly and accurately describes the effects of sin. That's about how ugly and messy things got for us.

DO NOT BE DECEIVED...

- Sin will take you further than you wanted to go.

  Sin is not usually an impulsive decision. It involves a process of deterioration. When you divert your affection from your spouse to another person, even in the smallest or slightest way, this is the first step in the blinding process that eventually leads to sin. It will always take you farther than you wanted to go.

- Sin will keep you longer than you wanted to stay.

  When we knowingly break God's laws, our hearts become hardened to the sin. When there are no immediate repercussions, you can be deceived into thinking that God has forgiven you and that there will be no consequences. You are sadly mistaken. I know I was.

- Sin will cost you more than you wanted to pay.

  Satan, the master deceiver, has a way of telling you, that you can do this and walk away...God will forgive you, and you will be fine. Let me assure you, the cost is great. The price is higher than you would ever want to pay. Sin won't ask for too much in the beginning, but in the end, it will steal everything you've got. Walk away from your sin right now, and close the door forever on this enemy of your marriage and soul.

Haggai 1:5 says, *"Now this is what the Lord Almighty says: 'Give careful thought to your ways.'"*

The *King James Version* says, "Consider your ways!" I want to encourage you to consider the consequences of being unfaithful to your spouse.

Allow me to share twenty-five of the consequences of my sin.

<u>**Relationships were damaged.**</u>

1. **My relationship with God.**
   The intimate communion I had known with God was broken. Now, I was experiencing His chastisement and correction. I still knew that God loved me, but my relationship had changed.

2. **My relationship with Starla.**
   I had hurt the person that I love the most. Now, my relationship with Starla would never be the same again. I promised to love and protect. I promised to be faithful to her. I had broken that trust and forever scarred our relationship. God has been faithful to heal and restore, but I should never have hurt my wife the way that I did.

3. **My relationship with my children.**
   I was supposed to be their hero and protector, but I had failed my children. What kind of an example is that? How would they ever trust me again? God has been faithful to heal and restore these relationships as well. Even so, it put a burden on my children that no child should ever have to carry.

4. **My relationship with the rest of my family.**
   It was horrible to look the rest of my family in the eyes and know that I had failed them as well.

5. **My relationship with my minister colleagues.**

   I realize that I made it more difficult on my colleagues. I caused their church families to have doubts and suspicions about their integrity.

6. **My relationship with my friends.**

   Many "friends" walked out and many "new friends" walked in, but it grieves me to know that I put people in that position.

7. **My relationship with my church family.**

   I let so many people down and hurt those who had put trust in me as their pastor. I was supposed to lead them by example and show them how to live for Jesus.

8. **My relationship with my community and neighbors.**

   I'll never forget the disappointing look on one of my neighbor's face. They didn't even go to church. This could possibly keep him from ever going to church or, more importantly, ever accepting Christ as his Savior.

9. **My relationship with people I had witnessed to.**

   There were people I had been witnessing to that may never come to Christ because of my sin.

10. **My relationship with people I had led to the Lord.**

    How disappointing it must be to know that the person who led you to Christ turned his back on Him and his own family for sin.

I experienced great loss. I lost...

11. **Trust.**

    Some people will never trust me again. I get it.

12. **Respect.**

    Some people will never respect me again.

13. **An unbroken love with my wife.**

    I can never get that back again.

14. **Friends.**

    There are certain friends that will never speak to me again.

15. **Souls.**

    There are people that will never make it into heaven because of what I did.

16. **Reputation.**

    Sometimes the only thing you have is your reputation. What do you do when that is lost?

17. **Dreams.**

    There are certain dreams that will never be fulfilled or realized now.

18. **A voice.**

    When you live in right standing with God, you have a certain voice to speak into people's lives. When you don't live in right standing with God, you lose that voice.

19. **A platform.**

    I had a platform to speak into people's lives. That platform was lost. God has restored a new platform, but the other is lost.

20. **Confidence.**

    There is a certain confidence that was lost for a long time.

21. **Income.**

    Our income was lost. We had to work very hard to rebuild what was lost. It was not easy.

22. **Happiness.**

    There was a season where we lost a lot of happiness. There was so much sadness that we had to look for opportunities to try to lift our spirits.

23. Celebration of certain events.

There were birthdays and anniversaries that were overshadowed by the heaviness of the storm we were in. We were unable to celebrate them properly. We will never get those special days back.

24. Self-image (Confidence).

Starla's self-image and mine were lost. God has done so much to restore, but for a long time, my self-image took such a hit that I was unable to believe in myself at all.

25. Opportunities.

There is no doubt that many opportunities that would have come our way were lost due to me compromising my marriage.

Galatians 6:7 says, "Do not be deceived: God cannot be mocked. A man reaps what he sows."

Habakkuk 1:13 says, "Your eyes are too pure to look on evil; you cannot tolerate wrongdoing."

Isaiah 59:2 says, "But your iniquities have separated you from your God; your sins have hidden His face from you, so that He will not hear."

I had one person tell me who was recovering from being unfaithful to his spouse, "If I had considered the consequences, I never would have done it." My hope, in sharing the consequences, is you will make up your mind to never make this selfish choice and open the door of temptation in your life. If you listen to my advice, you will be better.

19

(Kendall)
EMBRACE THE SHAME

"There is no need to be ashamed of tears, for tears bear witness that a man has the greatest courage, the courage to suffer."

— Victor Frankl

I'll never forget the first few weeks after our lives were turned upside, and I sat at home wondering what in the world I had done. How did I get myself into such a mess? How can I ever get out of this dark cave?

I received a phone call from a friend named Lorne Matthews. Lorne and his wife, Jimmie Ruth, had ministered at our church one time about how God had restored their marriage. It was a miraculous story. God was so awesome! He turned their lives around and now uses them to help others.

As he was talking to me and trying to encourage me, he said something that caught me completely off guard. He said, "Kendall, embrace the shame, just embrace the shame." I said, "Okay, I will." I didn't have a clue what he was talking about or what I was committing to. I was still in a very numb state, just trying to keep the spirit of depression and suicide off of me.

Around the same time frame, I read something that another minister had written. He said, "Don't talk about what you don't want people to remember." Now, I have to be completely honest with you. That sounded like better advice than, "Embrace the shame." The last thing in the world I wanted to do was tell everybody what I had done. I was hoping to get through it as quickly as possible, with as few people knowing as possible.

However, what Starla and I have found is great comfort, great reward, and great results from "embracing the shame." So many times I could have said nothing about my past, and no one would ever have known the difference. But because I opened up about my failures, God has opened doors for us that He never would have opened otherwise.

I remember meeting my next-door neighbor, here in Dallas, for the first time. We began to talk, and he asked me the question, "What brought you to Dallas?" I could have avoided it, but I chose to embrace the shame. I told him our story. He looked at me, kind of smiled, and said, "Where is your church? I want to go." He and his beautiful family have now been attending our church for the last eight years.

In fact, that is why we are writing this book. It's all part of "embracing the shame." I know that God is going to use this to help other people, marriages, and families who have walked through, or are walking through, the same devastation. God is faithful and will bring you through as well. He will give you the grace to get through.

2 Corinthians 12:9 says, "My grace is all you need." (NLT)

Believe me, I understand being ashamed. There was a period of many years that every time I walked into a room of other ministers, or of people that I knew, the only thing on my mind was, "I wonder if they are thinking of my failure?" The truth is it may still happen, but it's not the first thing on *my* mind when I walk into a room.

HERE IS WHAT "EMBRACE THE SHAME" REALLY MEANS.

1. **Embracing the shame doesn't mean you have to live in shame.**
   You are going to have to come out from underneath the cloud of shame at some time. If God has freed you, then you are free. You can't live in the past forever.

2. **Embracing the shame is recognizing the reality of the past in order to free someone for his or her future.**
   By embracing the shame and recognizing the reality of your past, you have the opportunity to help someone get free in order to achieve their very best

in the future. I believe God can turn our mistakes into miracles. I believe that He can take what the enemy meant for harm and turn it into something good.

Genesis 50:20 says, *"You intended to harm me, but God intended it for good to accomplish what is now being done, the saving of many lives."*

3. **Embracing the shame allows you to not hide from the past, but rather to thrive in spite of the past.**

   Just think of King David. His life is a blessing and an encouragement to us all, even though we know about the ugliest moments of his life. When King David cried out in Psalm 51, it was his moment of "embracing the shame."

   Psalm 51:10-13 says, *"10 Create in me a pure heart, O God, and renew a stead-fast spirit within me. 11 Do not cast me from Your presence or take Your Holy Spirit from me. 12 Restore to me the joy of Your salvation and grant me a willing spirit, to sustain me. 13 Then I will teach transgressors Your ways, so that sinners will turn back to You."*

Embracing the shame is about helping others.

Notice verses 12-13, David wanted to be restored so that he could help others. Embracing the shame is about helping others. If I didn't want to help others, I would take the other person's advice and never talk about what I don't want people to remember. But I would rather embrace the shame of my past in order to keep someone from doing the same.

20

(Kendall)
YOU CAN'T RUSH THE PROCESS

"When you are tempted to lose patience with someone, think how patient God has been with you all the time."

– UNKNOWN AUTHOR

I think the mistake that too many couples make when walking through the restoration of a broken marriage is trying to rush the process. I know the tendency is for the one who has offended to want the process to be completed as quickly as possible. They think, "The sooner the better." I know I did.

For the person who has been betrayed and offended, the healing takes more time. They are constantly conflicted between wanting to get past this and wanting to heal properly and completely. It's not easy.

There were three major indicators in the first year and a half of our restoration process that let me know this was not going to be quick, and it certainly was not going to be easy.

1. She couldn't commit to me that everything was going to be all right.
2. She couldn't wear the ring.
3. She couldn't say the vows.

LET ME EXPLAIN THESE THREE INDICATORS.

1. She couldn't commit to me that everything was going to be all right.
   Within the first few months of our "storm," we were invited to the home of a former pastor and his wife, who had been through the same thing

Starla and I were going through. This couple reached out to us and invited us to come stay with them in their home. They wanted to help us by sharing some of the things that helped them get through their "storm." I am deeply indebted to them for their kindness, compassion, and generosity.

We arrived, and the plan was to spend two days with them. They invited us into their lovely home. They both were so kind and courteous to us. They prayed with us, and we felt so encouraged. Then the pastor shared that the turning point in their marriage restoration was the moment when his wife took him by the hand and said, "Everything is going to be all right."

He looked Starla in the eyes and said, "Starla, can you take Kendall by the hand and tell him, 'Everything is going to be all right?'" She answered him very bluntly, "No, I can't. I'm not ready for that yet."

She then excused herself and called Dr. Richard Dobbins (our counselor) and told him the pressure that she was feeling at that moment. Dr. Dobbins told Starla to put me on the phone. I picked up the phone. He told me to kindly thank the couple for their consideration and excuse yourself, and inform them that you are taking your wife back home. She is not ready for this right now. Wow, that was awkward!

I was more committed to taking care of my wife than offending someone at that moment, so that's exactly what we did. There came a time that Starla was ready to make that kind of a commitment, but it wasn't that day. I had to be patient.

2. **She couldn't wear the ring.**

One year and four months into our restoration, I was allowed to start preaching again. We were invited to be guest speakers at different churches. Many times the pastor would lean over and ask me why Starla wasn't wearing a ring. I simply told them she wasn't ready yet. They always understood.

You see, after I confessed to Starla that I had been unfaithful to her, she took her ring off. I don't blame her. That ring represented vows that I had broken. It didn't mean the same anymore. I thought in time she would put it back on. She never did. I had to buy her a new one, which she soooo deserved.

3. **She couldn't say the vows.**

Sometime during the second year of our restoration, we were invited to speak at Journey Fellowship Church in Slidell, Louisiana. This is a church pastored by our good friends Pastors Doug and Rachael McAllister.

Annually, Journey Fellowship has a Renewal of the Vows Sunday, where all the couples stand and renew their vows to each other. This happened to be the Sunday that Doug had me speak. (I'm sure it was a set up by Pastor Doug to try to help.) At the conclusion of the message, I was to turn the service back over to Pastor Doug so he could lead the entire congregation in the renewal of their vows. While I was still speaking, Starla leaned over to Doug and said, "I'm not ready for this." He assured her she was under no pressure. However, while all the married couples in the church stood, joined hands, turned and faced each other, and repeated their vows to one another, Starla and I just sat and smiled.

I'm telling you these things because I want to be real about how we walked through this. It wasn't easy and was oftentimes awkward, but we were doing our best to be real with ourselves and with each other.

God didn't create the heavens and the earth in one moment or in a day. He needs time to work the healing process in broken hearts.

Did I ever wish that Starla would hurry up? Sure I did. I also recognized, though, that I was the one who had caused the injury to my precious wife. And I was willing to be as patient as I needed to be to allow her to heal properly. I made a promise to her that I would do whatever it took and wait as long as it took to try to repair what I had broken. I am still committed to that.

I also want to add that although Starla took a while to heal, I love the woman she has healed into. The woman that God has given birth to is an amazing woman of faith, and I am so proud to be married to her. I love you, Starla.

I had to learn that a healthy process of restoration required at least these three Keys.

1. **Patience!**

   You have to be willing to allow healthy healing to take place. Healthy healing will always take time. I know that God is able to do miracles in an instant. Let's face it, most of the time it takes time. God didn't create the heavens and the earth in one moment or in a day. He needs time to work the healing process in broken hearts.

2. **New start, new memories, new milestones.**

   Every new start needs to be commemorated with a new reminder. That's why God gave us the rainbow. We needed something that reminded us of a new start. I remember the day that Starla and I made our way to the jewelry store to pick out new wedding bands. It was as if we were engaged to be married all over again. We both purchased new rings that day. Every time I look at my new wedding band, I am reminded of a new beginning, a new start, a new marriage, and a new miracle.

3. **Be more committed to improving than impressing.**

   I know that there is a lot of pressure to try to save face and impress people. Forget all of that. Be more concerned about getting better than trying to impress people. Yes, it was awkward and embarrassing to walk away from someone's home. Yes, it was awkward and embarrassing for my wife to not wear her wedding band. Yes, it was awkward and embarrassing for Starla and me not to renew our vows while others did. But I had to be more committed to improving my marriage than impressing other people, and we are so much better today because of it.

21

(Kendall)
THE RESTORATION PROCESS

"The pain of discipline is nothing like the pain of disappointment."

– Justin Langer

I'm not going to lie: This was very hard. In the days following my confession, we were faced with the decision of what to do now. I had resigned from my church, but now we had to face whatever type of disciplinary action or restoration process I was willing to accept. It was my only hope of ever being involved in ministry again.

I had some independent pastor friends who offered a three-month process. I had others recommending a six-month to one-year process. I held ministerial credentials with the Assemblies of God, and their restoration process was two years. To be completely honest, that seemed like an eternity.

I had spent my whole life as an Assemblies of God minister. As I discussed the options with Starla, it was clear to me that she did not want me to try to take a shortcut through the restoration. Honestly, I wanted the easiest road, but I had determined that my first responsibility was to win the heart of my wife back. My national leaders, as well as my district leaders, were extremely compassionate to my family and me. However, the process was the process, and there would be no shortcuts. So I accepted the two-year process.

It was not an easy road. We initially relocated from Houston to Louisiana, so that meant I had to report to a different Ministerial Relations Committee. It's as if I had to start all over again. The humiliation only seemed to get worse. After seven months in Louisiana, we were going deeper and deeper into debt, unable to pay the bills. So out of desperation, to try to take care of my family, we relocated again to Dallas. The process started all over again with a new committee of ministers. The humiliation continued.

... each time you walk through the door of humility, you give God the chance to embrace you with His grace.

A wise pastor told me in so many words, "Don't avoid the door of humility. It may be painful and embarrassing to walk through, but each time you walk through the door of humility, you give God the chance to embrace you with His grace. His grace will get you through, and His grace will lift you up in due time."

1 Peter 5:6 says, "Humble yourselves, therefore, under God's mighty hand, that He may lift you up in due time."

In Dallas, we placed ourselves in a church under a pastor who embraced our broken family and gave us the healing we so desperately needed. I could never say thank you enough to Pastor J. Don and Gwen George for taking us in and being a part of our restoration process. They are heroes to me. I will forever be grateful.

We were also accountable to the North Texas District Superintendent Rick DuBose. Superintendent DuBose, his family, and team were always encouraging to my family and me. They welcomed us in and made us feel at home. Thank you, Superintendent DuBose, for taking a chance on us.

Since we had originally moved to Louisiana, Superintendent Doug Fulenwider oversaw our restoration process. So we continued to drive from Dallas to Louisiana for counseling and to report to the Ministerial Relations Committee. Superintendent Fulenwider and his team were awesome. They were not easy, but they were sincere. They were very thorough, and each time we would drive back to Louisiana, they would open the wounds and help us to process our pain. Ordinarily, the drive home was very difficult. More questions. More emotions. More processing. But we made it through.

Thank you, Superintendent Fulenwider, especially for the compassionate way that you ministered to my wife and daughters during this very difficult season. You'll never know how much that meant to us all.

Our General Superintendent, Dr. George Wood, is wise and gracious. He gave us great counsel and comfort along the way, as well as open arms when the process was completed. Dr. Wood, your spirit of encouragement was a breath of fresh air. You didn't have to allow us into the restoration process. I'm sure there were plenty of reasons not to. Thanks for giving me the chance to make things right, and thank you for allowing your team to walk through this with us.

I realize that as an Assemblies of God minister, I hurt the reputation of our fellowship with my failure. I had been entrusted with a great opportunity as a pastor of one of our fellowship's great churches, and I recklessly mishandled that privilege. It was my responsibility to uphold the standard of righteousness for our movement. I realize that my sin hurt not only my family, myself, and my local church, but the rest of the fellowship as well. My heart is continually grieved knowing this. I know I helped add to the doubt that some will have in trusting a pastor or church in the future. All of this constantly weighs heavy on my shoulders.

What did the process look like? For me it required weekly meetings with my supervising pastor and monthly meetings with my presbyter. There were also meetings every two months with the Ministerial Relations Committee. Counseling was at least every month for the first year. Monthly reports were turned in to my Superintendent, which entailed my daily devotional habits and personal journaling. Book reports were assigned, and I had to turn them in on a monthly basis.

I was not allowed to participate in any kind of ministry for the first year. During the second year I was allowed, under permission from my Superintendent, to begin ministering on occasion. At the conclusion of the two-year process, I was assessed, cleared, and reinstated as a minister in good standing with the Assemblies of God.

This is not an endorsement I take lightly. I appreciate the difficult two-year process I was subjected to. It showed me that our fellowship truly does value righteousness. They expect our ministers to live right. Thank you, Dr. Wood. Thank you to your team from the General Council, District Council, and the sections of the Assemblies of God. Thank you for valuing right living, restoration, and healing. My family is forever grateful.

Part 3:
Kendall and Starla's Chapters 22-26

22

(Kendall and Starla)
LET'S STAY TOGETHER

"If you don't stay together through the bad, then you won't be together for the good."

– CECILY MORGAN

The chorus in Al Green's song says, "Let's stay together, loving you whether, times are good or bad, happy or sad…" It's a very popular song that resonates with a lot of people who make the decision to fight for their marriages, rather than give up and go their separate ways. Love says, "I've seen the ugly parts of you, and I'm staying."

Love says, "I've seen the ugly parts of you, and I'm staying."

"How do you stay together no matter what? Number one: Stay together. Number two: No matter what." – Michael Xavier

Sounds pretty elementary right? It is not that easy. Staying together was one of the hardest decisions we have ever made. We had to take it one day at a time. Honestly, many of those days seemed hopeless.

We chose to stay together for several reasons:

1. For our Lord Jesus Christ
2. For each other
3. For our children
4. For others

FOR OUR LORD JESUS CHRIST

We have committed our lives to Christ first, above everything else. Everything that we do, easy or hard, has to be considered through the lens of what Jesus would want us to do. What would bring more glory and praise to our Lord? We believed that a restored marriage would honor God more than a broken one. We knew it wouldn't be easy. We knew it would be a fight and have its challenges, but we were willing to fight for what we really believed God wanted for us, not for what we wanted.

FOR EACH OTHER

We honestly believe that we are *better together*. We believe that we are *stronger together*. Yes, we could have walked a different path and possibly avoided some of the pain of restoration, but would we be as healed as we are today? No. We are confident that a restored marriage is much better than starting over. Many people carry the same unresolved issues into new relationships. When you work through a restoration process, you deal with the issues that caused the breakdown and become better and stronger than ever before.

FOR OUR CHILDREN

Our children deserve to see Mom and Dad willing to fight for what is best. We have heard it over and over again, "Children are resilient; they'll understand." What they understand is that Mom and Dad were not able to put their differences aside to do what was best for the family. Don't get us wrong; we know that there are times that starting over is the only option for some. We pray that God will give you the wisdom to know what is right.

As for our family, we decided we wanted to leave a legacy of restoration instead of a legacy of separation, so we decided to fight for our children. They didn't deserve to be torn apart and shuffled back and forth because their parents were unwilling to fight for what was better.

We have two amazing sons and two beautiful daughters-in-law. We have two gorgeous daughters and one handsome son-in-law. At this point, we have seven incredible grandchildren as well. We have pictures if you want to see!

We are all better because we were willing to fight for what was better.

FOR OTHERS

A few couples, who had walked through the pain and difficulty of restoring their marriage, reached out to us. They were strength and hope for us. Unfortunately, they were not enough. Too many couples choose to go their separate ways. We wanted to be able to give others the hope that God could heal and restore their marriages as well. We were sick and tired of seeing the devil destroy homes and tear families apart. We wanted to be able to tell the devil, "You didn't win this time. You tried, but you lost. You intended to harm and destroy us, but God is using our lives to help others."

Genesis 50:20 *says, "You intended to harm me, but God intended it for good to accomplish what is now being done, the saving of many lives."*

THE ROAD LESS TRAVELED

We understand that this is the road less traveled. We understand that divorce seems easier at the time. Sometimes it may be the only option, but it's often chosen out of revenge, anger and unforgiveness. It seems to be the way to make someone pay for what they have done. Other times, it is a way for someone to move on and live life with someone else that will "appreciate them and treat them the way they deserve." We don't fault anyone for that. Everyone deserves that, but for us, we believe God can use us better together. We believe that our story can be a help for others. We believe that the road less traveled, though paved with much pain and many trials, has a reward that cannot be experienced by taking any other way.

Why is this road so difficult? Because it takes a lot of dying to yourself. We both had to die to our own desires and humble ourselves before God and each other, in order for restoration to take place. We had to be willing to see a bigger picture. Remember what Jesus told His disciples.

Matthew **16:24-25** *says, "24 Then Jesus told his disciples, "If anyone would come after me, let him deny himself and take up his cross and follow Me. 25 For whoever would save his life will lose it, but whoever loses his life for My sake will find it." (ESV)*

There is a great reward in walking this road. Jesus said whoever loses his life for His sake will find it. We laid down our desires for the cause of Christ and found a much better life than we ever thought possible. Better is worth fighting for.

There are many questions or objections to staying together. Here are a few:

1. "But I am justified biblically to divorce."
2. "I don't deserve to be treated this way."
3. "I have no guarantee that it won't happen again."
4. "I can never trust again."
5. "I always said, 'This is one thing I would never forgive.'"

There are many valid reasons for not staying together; however, recovery is not an easy journey. That's why it's the road less traveled. You will face milestones along the road to recovery. Some will be easier to get past, and others will seem impossible. Some healings are immediate; others will take years. The cool thing is, even though it's a struggle, you'll see how liberating it is when you conquer your fears and get past the demons that have been haunting you. Your reward is freedom! With God, you can face and overcome anything!

One of the most beautiful things we've experienced during this journey of healing is:

1. Seeing the giants;
2. Facing the giants;
3. Plowing through the giants; and
4. Experiencing victory over the giants!

The crazy thing is, it wasn't impossible like we thought it would be. It wasn't near as scary as we thought it would be, and best of all, we came out on the other side stronger than we ever thought possible—closer to God and closer to each other, more in love with God and more in love with each other.

The truth is, if your desire is to follow Christ and to live a life that is pleasing to Him, you are already living on a road less traveled. Satan will be relentless in putting roadblocks before you your entire life. It will seem like quitting is easier because satan is very creative and good at deceiving us. On top of that, we humans are selfish and always want what is easier.

Please don't fall into this trap! Of course, it seems that taking a detour around the obstacles, turning around, or choosing another path will be less stressful. But don't forget that our journey is much more than plowing through bumps and roadblocks. Our journey is eternal. Every situation, every decision, and every reaction leads to your destiny.

You've probably heard of the "Butterfly Effect." It's the scientific theory that a single occurrence, no matter how small, can change the course of the universe forever. The flap of a butterfly's wings can change the air around it so much that a tornado can break out two continents away. Regardless of how accurate the theory is, it is provoking enough to cause us to stop and realize that every one of our decisions makes an eternal difference.

Our story has been much about the cascading effects of poor choices that brought us to and through the struggles we have shared. Now, consider the "Butterfly Effect" from a positive standpoint for a moment. What if we became more sensitive, more determined, and more intentional about every decision we make? What if we took into account the ripple effect our choices have on the rest of our lives and our eternal destination? What if we became so committed to evaluating every move we make with eternity in mind, rather than immediate gratification and satisfaction? What if we prayed every day, "God, don't let me make one selfish decision today. Let all of my thoughts, words, and actions honor and glorify You in every way possible?"

What if we went to bed each night considering ways that our lives, if given another opportunity to rise the next morning, could be invested in loving others, building them up, and encouraging the ones around us? What if we determined that every word we speak today would be uplifting, hopeful, and life giving? What if we brought every thought into alignment with God's Word and plan for our thought lives? What if, instead of putting this book down and saying this could never happen to me, you begin to believe that God—the Healer of broken wings and the Restorer of shattered dreams—can begin a miracle in your life today. If you will let Him begin, I promise He will complete it.

Philippians 1:6 *says, "Being confident of this, that He who began a good work in you will carry it on to completion."*

So, if God starts the work, we can be confident that He will complete it. Give God something to start with today. Your marriage can be *better*, if you stick it out. It may take a few years to turn the corner, and you'll have struggles along the way. There will need to be major adjustments for sure, but in the long run, a better marriage is in your future, if you are willing to fight for it and stay together.

Now let's all sing Al Green's song, "Let's Stay Together!" Come on, you know you want to.

23

(Kendall and Starla)
MAN IN THE MIRROR

"You have to get along with people, but you also have to recognize that the strength of a team is different people with different perspectives and different personalities."

– STEVE CASE

Rather than accepting and supporting one another, we spent more time trying to change each other. Bad idea! One of the biggest mistakes couples make when they get married is trying to change their spouse. The crazy thing is it was those "differences" that attracted you to each other in the first place.

You put up with each other's differences while dating, but somehow think that once you are married, you have the right or obligation to modern civilization to change him or her. You have wrong and unrealistic expectations. If your goal is to change your spouse, you will always be frustrated.

Men and women are different. Just think of these three areas alone:

GENDER SPECIFICS (MAN AND WOMAN)
Men are like microwaves, and women are like crockpots. When it comes to getting ready in the morning, packing for a trip, deciding what to wear, buying Christmas gifts, or sex, men are like microwaves—the faster the better. Women are like crockpots—the slower the better. They want it to be perfect, and you can't change that.

Some things just aren't going to change. Your best bet is to *understand* that men and women are wired differently for different things.

PERSONALITIES

There is usually a difference in our personalities. We are all made differently. Please remember that. We are *made* this way. To try to change the other person is only going to frustrate you both. It is possible for each spouse to have the same personality. There is no right or wrong. The failure comes in not understanding each other's personalities, which explain why a person does what they do. They're wired that way. It's their God-given personality.

We are no personality experts, but we have done enough personality profiles to know we are opposites. We are *extreme* opposites. For years, we allowed those differences to be the reason we were frustrated with each other. Trying to change each other only led to major headaches in our relationship, but the glaring truth we both missed for so long was that our differences complimented each other perfectly. Where one was strong, the other may be weak. Where one was weak, the other would be strong. How divine is that? But rather than help each other along the way, we spent too much time trying to change one another. Truthfully, if we were both the same, then one of us would be unnecessary.

(Pick up a copy of, *Personality Plus: "How to Understand Others by Understanding Yourself,"* by Florence Littauer.)

LOVE LANGUAGES

We love what we have learned by reading, *The Five Love Languages*, by Gary Chapman. When you finally understand how you and your spouse give and receive love, it will make a world of difference in your marriage.

When it's all said and done, the most important, impactful, and life-changing love language of all is *dying to self.*

It is possible for you to express love extravagantly in *your* love language, but if love is not communicated in your *spouse's* love language, all of your effort is for nothing. It would be like speaking to your spouse in Spanish when he or she only speaks English. You could tell him you love him all day long, but he would never know it because you're not speaking a language he understands.

Again, each person has a different love language. You can't change your spouse's love language, but you can understand it. It may be possible that you and your spouse share the same love language. That's awesome. But you still need to know what it is in order to communicate love in a way that it is given and received.

(Pick up a copy of, "*The Five Love Languages,*" by Gary Chapman.)

When it's all said and done, the most important, impactful, and life-changing love language of all is *dying to self.* Doing so is what we need in order for our marriages to be what God wants them to be. This is not one of the five love languages that you will read about in Gary Chapman's book. It's found in the following verse:

Galatians 5:24 says, "*Those who belong to Christ Jesus have nailed the passions and desires of their sinful nature to His cross and crucified them there.*" *(NLT)*

As fully devoted followers of Christ, we must nail the passions and desires of our sinful nature to His cross and crucify them there. Put them to death, so that you can live the *better life* God has in store for you. When you begin to focus on *understanding* rather than *changing,* we are certain you can make your marriage so much better. In fact, it will allow you to stop fighting each other and begin fighting the enemy—the one who is trying to destroy your family (**John 10:10**).

We recommend that you take the personality test, take the love language test, and find out what makes you and your spouse so unique. Then, start working together for a better future. We believe that God's plan for you is so much better than anything that you have realized. We believe that the reason you are under such an attack right now is because satan is trying to destroy what God has prepared for you.

Read this verse below.

1 Corinthians 2:9 says, "*No eye has seen, no ear has heard, and no mind has imagined what God has prepared for those who love him.*" *(NLT)*

What God has prepared for you is bigger and better than you have ever imagined. It is worth fighting for. It's worth the prayers. It's worth taking the stand. We know what it's like to lose almost everything except our marriage. But when we took our stand and refused to allow satan to have our marriage, God's dream for our family emerged. And His plan was so much bigger and better than we ever dreamed.

Here's where you can start.

INSTEAD OF TRYING TO CHANGE YOUR SPOUSE, WHY NOT TRY TO CHANGE YOURSELF?

1. **Change the way you think.**

   Proverbs 23:7 says, *"For as he thinks in his heart, so is he."* (NKJV)

   Quit thinking about failure, revenge, hurts, and pain. Instead, think about all the things that God has done for you. Think about the dreams and plans He has for you and your family. This may sound easier said than done, but you have to take control of your thoughts because no one else will. If you allow the enemy to fill your mind with negative thoughts, it will take you down a destructive path. The real battlefield begins in your mind with your thoughts.

   We both had to change the way we thought. We had a lot of "stinkin' thinkin'," but when we took control of our thoughts, we took control of our lives.

2. **Change the way you speak.**

   Proverbs 18:21 says, *"The tongue has the power of life and death."*

   You must speak words of life. Quit speaking words of death over your spouse and marriage. We know you may feel like telling them where they can go and what they can do, but none of that is pretty. We know you may not feel like speaking positively right now, and we understand there's a process that takes time. But you cannot allow your words to sabotage your future and your healing process. Choose words that encourage and affirm. Find the good and talk about it. Refuse to allow negative talk to dominate your conversation. Your words have the power of life and death.

3. Change the way you act.

John 13:34 says, *"Love one another, as I have loved you."*

Love is a verb. It requires action. In order to truly fulfill the command of Christ to love one another, you must act on it. This may be the most difficult thing you ever do, but in order to change your circumstances, you must express love regardless of how you may feel.

We know what it is like to not want to "love" each other. Sometimes, it just came more naturally to fight. There were times we would fight and argue over the silliest and most insignificant things in the world. But when you are not intentionally choosing to express love, the enemy has a way of throwing distractions in your way to derail you from the beauty of being together. You have to be able to move from *me* to *we*.

I know we live in a world that celebrates individualism and independence, but in order for your marriage to be better, there has to be more *we* than *me*. You have to find ways to do things together and get on the same team. You have to start acting like you did when you were dating, crazy in love with each other. You did everything together.

If your marriage is in trouble right now, I know this doesn't sound very appealing. You have probably grown apart and have your own schedules and individual lives. Ask yourself this question: "Which comes first—a better marriage or activities that bring you together?" Obviously, activities that bring you together are what create a better marriage. You must work on the activities that will bring you together long before you feel like it.

We love spending time together, whether it is camping, hiking, exercising, shopping for antiques, waterskiing, or hanging out on the beach. We have found a lot of activities we really enjoy doing together. We still have individual interests that the other does not participate in, but we make sure our time together dominates our time apart.

Do not let satan win! Change yourself, and you can change your world.

Mother Teresa said, "If everyone only cleaned their own doorstep, the whole world would be clean."

"I Wanted to Change the World" by Unknown Monk, 1100 A.D.

When I was a young man, I wanted to change the world.
I found it was difficult to change the world, so I tried to change my nation.
When I found I couldn't change the nation, I began to focus on my town. I couldn't change the town, and as an older man, I tried to change my family.
Now, as an old man, I realize the only thing I can change is myself, and suddenly I realize that if long ago I had changed myself, I could have made an impact on my family. My family and I could have made an impact on our town. Their impact could have changed the nation, and I could indeed have changed the world.

So what can *you* do to change *yourself*?

24

(Kendall and Starla)
WE'RE ON THE SAME TEAM

"Alone we can do so little; together we can do so much."

– HELEN KELLER

We were living in the same house, just not on the same page. We were working together in one church, just not toward the same goal. We were raising the same children, just not with a unified effort. Don't get us wrong. We weren't ignoring or not speaking to each other. We just weren't on the same team.

Too often, couples view themselves as competitors rather than teammates. In fact, many couples make small, and what seem like, insignificant decisions that separate rather than unite. Have you realized that there is a very small difference between the words "unite" and "untie?" Yet, they mean completely different things and are total opposites. If you simply reverse the two letters, "i" and "t," you get two different words, with two different meanings.

The same is true in a marriage relationship. Oftentimes, you only have to adjust a few things to get a totally different outcome. Check out these ten steps that you can take to "un*ite*" rather than "un*tie*."

STEP 1 - MOVE FROM SELFISHNESS TO SELFLESSNESS.

Notice again how much these words sound alike, but how different their meanings are. We both came into the marriage extremely selfish. We went from fighting for our own way to learning how to put each other's needs first. It requires a lot of give and take, but if each one is committed to putting the other first, everyone wins. Sometimes it helps to assign days for who gets to decide and who gets to break the tie.

When our sons were younger, they competed against each other for everything, from getting ready in the morning, to sports, to who finished their meal first. Everything was a competition. Who got to ride in the front seat of the car on the way to school was a competition. So we finally assigned days. Monday and Wednesday belonged to one. Tuesday and Thursday belonged to the other. We alternated Fridays. Now, everyone was happy and all was fair. There was no more competition, at least in the car on the way to school. You can do the same thing in your marriage.

STEP 2 - FIGHT FAIR

We don't really like this term because the word fight implies, screaming, yelling, and throwing things. That should never be the case, but there needs to be understood guidelines for disagreeing or arguing in a mature way. Every couple will inevitably have a difference of opinion on any number of things in life.

Here are some rules for fighting fair.

A. **In the end, both must win.**
   If one wins, the other loses. That leads to resentment. There must be enough negotiation and compromise that both spouses take away something positive or win.

B. **Have an agreed upon time and place.**
   Never fight in front of your children. Never fight when you are so mad that you can't think straight. You may both need a time to cool off in order to think clearly. Choose a time and a place that allows for each person to physically and emotionally prepare. It is unwise to fight when one or both are so tired and exhausted that you can't make rational decisions. That's when

emotions get out of control, and things are said and done that are not helpful to the issue.

C. Stick to the subject.

Don't use this as an opportunity to bring up every issue that you have ever had in your marriage. You can talk about the toilet seat, the toothpaste cap, and the time it takes to get ready at another time and place.

D. You may need a mediator, counselor, or coach.

We did. It took a marriage counselor to help us learn how to "hear" each other and how to "speak to be heard."

E. Be respectful.

You may have lost respect for your spouse, but that doesn't give you the right to be disrespectful. Speak in a mature way that allows your hurts to be clearly heard. Don't assume your spouse understands. You probably wouldn't be where you are right now if you were understood. Don't use the confidential knowledge of your spouse's weaknesses or insecurities to hit below the belt. Be bigger than that.

F. Choose your words wisely.

Don't use words that you don't *really mean*, even though you *really feel* them at the moment. This is why "cooling off" is a good thing. Don't use hateful, harmful, and hurtful words, but rather use words that heal and help. You are fighting to find common ground and a solution, not to injure and repay evil for evil.

G. Always give feedback and review.

Say to one another, "I think this is what I am hearing you say...(repeat back what you heard)." Then ask, "Is that right?" This always gives an opportunity for you to clear the differences between man's language and woman's language. It's amazing how many times we thought we heard what the other was saying, but interpreted it incorrectly.

H. Give adequate time for expression.

Never conclude a discussion without each agreeing that they were heard. Each person needs the opportunity to express himself or herself and be heard.

I. Agree on "next steps."

You may not completely agree on the subject of discussion, but you can agree on the next step you will take to move forward. The longer the issue remains unresolved, the worse it becomes.

J. Pray.

Prayer always helps. In fact, you should agree that your fights, arguments, or discussions will always begin and/or end in prayer. It is amazing, but most will find it very difficult to pray for one another while they're still mad. Prayer has a way of forcing us to submit to God and to one another. That's a good thing.

STEP 3 - AGREE ON FINANCES

You both need to be on the same page and team when it comes to money. I know many couples operate with a, "what's yours is mine and what's mine is mine," mentality. That's never going to unite a marriage. It doesn't matter who is providing the income. You are both participating to make this marriage work.

It's as simple as:

- Having an agreed upon budget.
- Deciding together how the money will be spent each month.
- Having open and honest transparency about your money. (This also provides a measure of accountability that everyone needs.)

Remember you are on the same team. No one person should decide how *all* of the money is spent *all* of the time. Do it together, work together, and you'll be better.

STEP 4 - ESTABLISH BOUNDARIES

You need to agree on boundaries in the following areas.

A. Relationships.

This is most important with members of the opposite sex. For us, being alone with someone of the opposite sex is not an option. This can also apply to all friends. Agree on how much time is acceptable to be with other friends. This needs to be a win/win.

B. In-Laws.

Decide how much time is to be spent with each other's family and how much information is to be shared with them. You may be able to forgive your spouse, but your family may not. Be careful how much you share with your family.

C. Social Media (Phone and Computer).

For complete trust and transparency, you do not need to have secrets or limit access; everything needs to be shared with your spouse. Secrecy only breeds distrust. Knowing each other's passwords is another key to being transparent. While we are on technology, put the phones down when you are spending time together. Be present in the moment.

D. Work.

How much time is acceptable to be at work and away from home? Every family is different. Each person's needs are different. This should be understood long before you enter into a marriage relationship. Some careers will require more time away than others.

E. Play/Hobbies.

How much time is acceptable for each person to be away enjoying hobbies or extra-curricular activities? How many of these activities can you do together? Find ways to unite.

STEP 5 - ACTIVE ROMANCE

Make time to be together and meet each other's needs. Make time to love your "one and only." The busier your lives get, the more planned this will need to become. Don't let this slip through the cracks. Part of your marriage responsibility is meeting this need.

STEP 6 - HEALTHY COMMUNICATION

We cannot stress enough the importance of taking time to communicate. Yes, we communicate differently, but we still communicate. This takes some patience, but it is so worth it when you get on the same team.

Choose words of life—words that heal and give hope. You may also need to identify some words you will never speak to each other. Understanding each other's love languages and personalities is a great help as well. Another valuable tool in healthy communication is learning to listen and listen well.

STEP 7 - HONESTY

Be open and honest about what you want in a marriage. Express your dreams and desires. Be honest about how things make you feel. Too many couples don't honestly express how they feel about their spouse's behaviors until it reaches a boiling point. Be honest about what you love in each other and about what concerns you. Then work together for something better.

STEP 8 - TEAMWORK

We all face challenges in life such as: sickness, job loss, infertility, miscarriages, business failures, etc. Challenges come to us all. In those moments, we must find ways to encourage, strengthen, and build one another up, rather than tear each other down, cast blame, or crawl into an emotional hole.

There will be times when one of you will be weak, and the other needs to be strong. The time will come when the tables are turned. We have found by coming together that teamwork makes impossible situations possible. Regardless of how painful it was, we found that we are better together through the challenges we have faced. You can be too.

STEP 9 - TIME

There is a big difference between *quantity* of time and *quality* of time. Some say, "I don't have a lot of time to give, but what I give is quality." In a good marriage relationship, it's not really an either/or decision. It's both. Your relationship needs both quantity and quality. You can spend a lot of time together, but if it isn't quality time, it doesn't unite. You can spend quality time together, but if it isn't in proper quantity, it doesn't unite.

You've probably heard of the older man who was rummaging through old boxes in his attic. He came across an old tattered journal that belonged to his son. He opened it and read about life through the eyes of his child. He then remembered that he had kept a journal himself and wondered if his memory of those days were the same as his son's. He opened his journal next to his son's. His eyes fell on a certain day in his own journal. It stood out because of the brevity of the entry. It read, "Wasted the whole day fishing with Jimmy. Didn't catch a thing." He opened up Jimmy's journal to the same day, and it read, "Went fishing with my Dad. It was the best day of my life."

Quantity *and* quality are both needed for better relationships.

We love spending time and doing things—together. We enjoy life together. Our time is quality and quantity. It makes life better.

STEP 10 (THE MOST IMPORTANT STEP OF ALL) - DESIRE TO SEE YOUR SPOUSE BECOME EVERYTHING GOD CREATED HIM OR HER TO BE.

Make it your greatest goal in life to see your husband or wife become the man or woman of God they are destined to be.

Make it your greatest goal in life to see your husband or wife become the man or woman of God they are destined to be. Make sure that your spouse is spiritually healthy. You have a spiritual responsibility to one another.

Ephesians 5:21 says, "And further, submit to one another out of reverence for Christ." (NLT)

Both husband and wife have a responsibility to make the marriage what God intended it to be.

Look at the following lists of biblical roles for the husband and wife. See if you notice the *one common role*.

THE HUSBAND'S ROLE IN MARRIAGE

1. **Lead His Wife**

   1 Corinthians 11:3 says, "But I want you to realize that the head of every man is Christ, and the head of the woman is man, and the head of Christ is God."

2. **Love His Wife**

   Ephesians 5:25 says, "Husbands, love your wives, just as Christ loved the church and gave Himself up for her."

3. **Serve His Wife**

   John 3:1-17 (Jesus' example of washing His disciple's feet)

   Philippians 2:7 says, "Rather, He made Himself nothing by taking the very nature of a servant, being made in human likeness."

4. **Provide For His Wife**

   Ephesians 5:23 says, "For the husband is the head of the wife as Christ is the head of the church, His body, of which He is the Savior." (Savior means "provider of all things.")

THE WIFE'S ROLE IN MARRIAGE

1. **Help Her Husband**

   Genesis 2:18 says, "The Lord God said, "It is not good for the man to be alone. I will make a helper suitable for him."

2. **Respect Her Husband**

    Ephesians 5:33 *says, "However, each one of you also must love his wife as he loves himself, and the wife must respect her husband."*

3. **Love Her Husband**

    Titus 2:4 *says, "Then they can urge the younger women to love their husbands and children."*

4. **Submit to Her Husband**

    Ephesians 5:22 *says, "Wives, submit yourselves to your own husbands as you do to the Lord."*

According to the lists above, only one role is duplicated, and that is the responsibility to **love your spouse**. There is a big difference between the love that we experience in courtship—emotional love that consumes us and literally blinds us to the realities of whom we are dating—and the love that sustains a marriage for years to come (the attitude of love). One is *emotional*; the other is an *attitude*. One *drives* you; the other must be *driven*. One *commands* you; the other you must *command*.

The beautiful thing is, once the emotional love wears off and you get down to "real life," you can operate in the right "attitude of love," and the emotions will follow. It is possible to stay in love for a lifetime. You just have to make the right choice.

If you are thinking, "I just don't know if I can do this," remember this: God will never require you to do anything that He will not enable you to do. God wants your marriage *better*.

"A newspaper columnist named George Crane once told of a woman who was full of hatred toward her husband. Someone counseled the woman to act as if she really loved

her husband, to tell him how much he meant to her, to praise him for every decent trait, to be kind, considerate, and generous whenever possible. Then, when she'd fully convinced him of her undying love, she'd make her move and file for divorce. With revenge in her eyes she said, "That's perfect, I'll do it." And so she did...but guess what happened... the more she demonstrated sacrificial love toward her husband, the more she began to actually love him, and at the end of a few months divorce was the furthest thing from her mind." (Illustration shared by Timothy Peck, Life Bible Fellowship Church, February 2001)

You see, when you activate the *attitude* of love, the *emotion* will follow. You may ask, "Is that really possible?" We are living proof that it is. God did it for us, and He can do it for you.

25

(Kendall and Starla)
AGAINST ALL ODDS

"Our broken marriage didn't begin with broken vows. It began with our broken lives."

— Kendall and Starla

The odds were stacked against us from the start. Don't get us wrong; we aren't blaming anyone but ourselves. We had every opportunity to start right, strong, and healthy. We just didn't take advantage of the resources that were available to us. We didn't take our marriage or commitment seriously enough.

We were young, selfish, and un-teachable. We were unwilling to take the blame or get help. We didn't know how to communicate, and we let it drive us apart. We didn't need counseling. In addition, Jesus wasn't first. We could go on and on, but we think you get the point. Our marriage was a recipe for disaster. We let satan have a foothold, and he got the best of us.

Ephesians 4:27 says, *"Do not give the devil a foothold."*

We realize this scenario isn't unique to us. Most couples begin their marriages at a disadvantage, and satan takes advantage of that. He uses our weaknesses to drive us further apart and create separation between one another and us and our God. Satan has been doing this since the beginning of time. He started attacking marriages in the beginning, as soon as God established the first one. You probably remember the story.

God created Adam and Eve and placed them in the beautiful Garden of Eden. With the exception of one tree, He gave them full rule and reign over everything the garden had to offer. God said, "Do not eat of this tree. You can have everything else in the garden, just don't touch this one." As soon as God left Adam and Eve alone, satan came to Eve and deceived and confused her. He told Eve, "God doesn't want you to eat of that tree because you will be like Him. God is holding out on you." They both believed the lie and ate of the tree's fruit.

When God came to Adam and asked, "Did you eat of the tree?" Adam blamed Eve, and she blamed the serpent. Instead of accepting responsibility, they both blamed someone else. The very first sin that satan convinced Adam and Eve to commit drove a wedge in their marriage. They refused to accept the blame.

This shouldn't surprise us. The Bible tells us that we have an enemy who is set out to destroy us. Satan's plan has always been to divide and destroy the marriage union.

1 Peter 5:8 says, "Be alert and of sober mind. Your enemy the devil prowls around like a roaring lion looking for someone to devour."

The devil hates you, your marriage, and the God in you. He hates the fact that marriage is a symbol of the gospel of Jesus.

Ephesians 5:31-32 says, "31 For this reason a man will leave his father and mother and be united to his wife, and the two will become one flesh. 32 This is a profound mystery—but I am talking about Christ and the church."

Did you know that God has a plan for your life and marriage? Without a doubt! God's plans for our lives began before we were even born.

Jeremiah 1:5 says, "Before I formed you in the womb I knew you, before you were born I set you apart; I appointed you as a prophet to the nations."

Jeremiah 29:11 says, "For I know the plans I have for you," declares the Lord, "plans to prosper you and not to harm you, plans to give you hope and a future."

Satan's plans to destroy and defeat God's plan in your life began the moment you were born.

God wants you to succeed in life and, most importantly, in your marriage. He wants your marriage to be a testimony to the world of how the relationship between Jesus Christ and His followers works. Jesus laid down His life for all men, even before we were born. He showed unconditional love to us all. He sacrificed completely for our benefit, and He still makes intercession for us. When our marriages are patterned after the blueprint Jesus demonstrated for us, we can be assured that God will bless and protect our marriages.

Did you know that satan also has a plan for your life and marriage?

"Don't think of satan as a harmless cartoon character with a red suit and a pitch-fork. He is very clever and powerful, and his unchanging purpose is to defeat God's plans at every turn—including His plans for your life." — Billy Graham

Satan's plans to destroy and defeat God's plan in your life began the moment you were born.

SATAN WANTS TO DEFEAT YOU WITH:

1. **Doubt** – Satan will try to get you to doubt God and doubt His plan for your life.

   John 20:27 says, "Jesus said, "Stop doubting and believe."

2. **Division** – Satan will try to drive a wedge between you and God and you and your spouse. He will use any minor or major thing to divide you. But when

you choose to be unified, you have the power of Almighty God working on your behalf.

Romans 16:17 says, *"I urge you, brothers and sisters, to watch out for those who cause divisions and put obstacles in your way that are contrary to the teaching you have learned. Keep away from them."*

3. **Disappointment** – Satan will make his best effort to cause you to be disappointed in God and your spouse. You must realize that God loves you more than anything and certainly more than you realize. He wants only good for your life.

Romans 8:28 says, *"And we know that for those who love God all things work together for good, for those who are called according to his purpose."* (ESV)

4. **Discouragement** – If satan can get a foothold in your life and marriage, he will work his way in and begin his discouraging and destructive process.

Psalm 42:11 says, *"Why, my soul, are you downcast? Why so disturbed within me? Put your hope in God, for I will yet praise Him, my Savior and my God."*

Ephesians 4:27 says, *"Do not let the devil start working in your life."* (NLV)

God's plan for your marriage is simple:

1. Unity
2. Shared purpose
3. Safe and healthy family environment
4. Encouraging
5. Fulfilling
6. Rewarding
7. Helpmate
8. Faithful

9. Unselfish love

10. Commitment to the vows/promises

Satan's plan for your marriage is deadly, satanic:

1. Divorce

2. Division

3. Divided purpose

4. Fear

5. Unhealthy family environment

6. Discouraging

7. Unfulfilling

8. Unfaithful

9. Selfish

10. Broken vows/promises

Here's the bottom line: Approximately 50 percent of all marriages end in divorce.

The main reasons are:

1. Communication

2. Finances

3. Abuse

4. "Fell out of love"

5. Infidelity

The likelihood of divorce drastically increases each time you remarry. 60 percent of second marriages and 73 percent of third marriages end in divorce. Therefore, you must guard your relationship with God, your marriage, your spouse, and your family. This is war. But the good news is, with God's help, you will win.

1 John 4:4 says, "*You, dear children, are from God and have overcome them, because the one who is in you is greater than the one who is in the world.*"

Isaiah 54:17 *says, "No weapon formed against you shall prosper." (NKJV)*

Romans 8:37 *says, "No, in all these things we are more than conquerors through Him who loved us."*

There are no perfect marriages or perfect people. There is a perfect God who can take our imperfections and brokenness and make all things better.

We pray that God would help you win this battle against your marriage. We know that it is a tough road, but what doesn't kill you makes you stronger, right? We are definitely stronger. We are definitely better. Who knew God could take brokenness and shattered dreams and make something better? But He did for us, and He will for you.

We speak healing to your brokenness. We speak hope to your hopelessness. We speak unity to your division. We speak peace in the midst of your chaos. We declare that the God whom you serve is bigger than the enemy who is attacking your life and marriage right now.

We declare that out of the ashes of your pain will rise a beautiful story of restoration, healing, and strength to continue to move forward and upward to the better place God has for you.

26

(Kendall and Starla)
MINISTRY AGAIN WITH A MASK-OFF APPROACH

"If you are honest, truthful and transparent, people trust you. If people trust you, you have no grounds for fear, suspicion or jealousy."

— AZGRAY BEBLY JOSLAND

We wondered if we would ever be used in ministry again. Our dreams had been crushed. Our hearts were broken, but God is the Healer of the brokenhearted.

Psalm 34:18 says, *"The Lord is **close to the brokenhearted**; He **rescues those whose spirits are crushed."** (NLT)*

That was us! So we knew that God was near and had begun to rescue us. After a few years passed, God allowed us to begin to dream again. You can't imagine what it

We made a decision that if the time ever came to plant another church, we would do ministry differently than before.

was like to just dream, to imagine, being able to say with some measure of hope, "What if?" After being in a dark cave of doubt and uncertainty for so long, we were beginning to see a glimmer of light, a ray of hope. We felt that God was calling us to plant another church.

We called our family together into our living room. We wanted to pray with them and ask if they felt the same as we did. We prayed and shared our dream to plant a church in Dallas. It was such a miraculous night. God was so very present that evening. There were prophetic words of confirmation that were spoken, and everyone agreed that it was the Lord's will.

We made a decision that if the time ever came to plant another church, we would do ministry differently than before. We cannot tell you how refreshing it is to do ministry with a mask-off approach. We know the pressure of living in the fishbowl, the glass house, always under the microscope of everyone watching. There was this pressure of trying to live up to people's expectations of what they thought we were supposed to be. So we had a tendency to try to keep the mask on in order to appear that we were the perfect couple with the perfect family building the perfect church. Ha! None of that really exists anywhere. I don't know why we pretend that it does.

The truth is we really enjoy the having the pressure removed. It enables us to open up our wounds and show our scars. When we tell people what we have been through, we know that it disqualifies us from some, but it qualifies us for others. And that's alright because we know we aren't called to *everyone*, but we are called to *certain ones*.

Not too long ago, a lady in our church came to us and said that a woman from another church in our town asked her how she could go to a church and sit under a pastor, knowing that he had been unfaithful to his wife. Obviously, we are disqualified from ministering to this woman and others I'm sure, but you know what? There are a ton of couples that are trying to find a way to save their marriages from going under. These couples need someone who understands what they are going through. They need someone to be real, someone who has scars. They need someone who is not going to look down on them for their failures, or stiff-arm them from getting too close. They need someone who will embrace them and walk with them. They need someone who realizes *all* sin hurts our Lord Jesus. The sin of gossip hurts our Lord, as well as the sin of adultery.

Isn't it surprising how we categorize sin? We measure certain sins as socially acceptable, mostly in the church circles, but others we do not accept. How gutless, shallow, and pretentious we are. Come on...let's call it like it is. Sin is sin, and it all bears the penalty of death.

Romans 6:23 says, "For the wages (penalty) of sin is death, but the gift of God is eternal life in Christ Jesus our Lord."

In fact, the Bible makes it pretty clear that all these sins listed below will keep us out of the Kingdom.

1 Corinthians 6:9-10 says, "9 Don't you realize that those who do wrong will not inherit the Kingdom of God? Don't fool yourselves. Those who indulge in sexual sin, or who worship idols, or commit adultery, or are male prostitutes, or practice homosexuality, 10 or are thieves, or greedy people, or drunkards, or are abusive, or cheat people—none of these will inherit the Kingdom of God." (NLT)

That's a pretty broad list, from greedy cheaters to the sexually immoral. What about this next list?

Galatians 5:19-21 says, "19 When you follow the desires of your sinful nature, the results are very clear: sexual immorality, impurity, lustful pleasures, 20 idolatry, sorcery, hostility, quarreling, jealousy, outbursts of anger, selfish ambition, dissension, division, 21 envy, drunkenness, wild parties, and other sins like these. Let me tell you again, as I have before, that anyone living that sort of life will not inherit the Kingdom of God." (NLT)

Hostility to sorcery, anger to division—we all get nailed at some point. So, if you are going to point out the speck in someone's eye, get ready to pull the log out of your own.

Matthew 7:3 says, "And why worry about a speck in your friend's eye when you have a log in your own?" (NLT)

Now, we're not saying to go light on sin. Not at all. But let's be quick to restore, not quick to condemn. Isn't that what Jesus taught us when He told the woman caught in adultery to go and sin no more?

John 8:11 says, "Neither do I condemn you; go and sin no more." (NKJV)

The Bible teaches us that our ministry is to restore people to Christ, not to hold their sins against them.

2 Corinthians 5:19 says, *"God was in Christ reconciling the world to Himself, not counting people's sins against them [but canceling them]. And He has committed to us the message of reconciliation [that is, restoration to favor with God]."* (AMP)

What we are trying to communicate is that according to **Romans 3:23**, "All have sinned and fall short of the glory of God." We have all missed the mark at some point. *Let's quit operating in so much condemnation, but rather in restoration.* The best way to do that is to take the mask off, show your scars, get real, and commit to be a part of the healing process in others' lives.

Where we are now? We pastor Freedom Church in Carrollton, Texas (www.findfreedom.church). Carrollton is a suburb of Dallas. We chose the name because of the freedom we have experienced in walking through this process of restoration. We have freedom from the strongholds that hindered our marriage. We have freedom in Jesus Christ. Our statement of purpose is, "Helping People Find Freedom." We truly want to help others find this same freedom in Christ. This is the main reason we have opened up our lives to share our deepest pain and our greatest struggles. We believe that in doing so we can help people find freedom.

We love the people of Freedom Church. They have accepted us just as we are—scars, wounds, hurts, failures, brokenness, and all. We don't pretend to be anything that we are not. We love helping them through the same struggles and giving them hope that God can, and will, make their lives better. And He will do the same for you.

All four of our children and their families are involved in the church ministry in some capacity or another. Talk about restoration! That is a miracle! We fought for our children, and God is using them all in the ministry. Take that, devil!

So what does ministry with a mask-off approach look like?

Remember Star Trek and the mission of the original Starship Enterprise? (The following must be read with a William Shatner voice.) *"Space: the final frontier. These are the voyages of the Starship Enterprise. Its five-year mission: to explore strange new worlds, to seek out new life and new civilizations, to boldly go where no man has gone before."*

That's the way we felt launching into ministry again with a "mask-off approach"—going where no man has gone before. Don't get us wrong, we know we are not the only ones attempting to do ministry differently. There are a lot of great ministries keeping it real, but it was new territory for us.

HERE IS A SIMPLE DESCRIPTION OF WHAT WE THINK MINISTRY WITH A MASK-OFF APPROACH SHOULD LOOK LIKE.

1. **Transparency** – Opening up your heart, your life, your scars, and your wounds. Letting people see in—the good, the bad, and the ugly.

2. **Honesty** – Being real about yourself, others, and the struggles we all face.

3. **Vulnerability** – Not being afraid to show others our weaknesses and allow them to see when we hurt.

4. **Judgment-Free Zone** – People need time to become like Christ. First, you catch the fish, then you clean them, not the other way around.

5. **Love Without Limits** – Loving people just the way they are.

6. **Be Human** – We don't try to pretend that we are superheroes.

7. **Relate to Others Where They are** – We understand that everyone has issues that they are dealing with. We meet them right there.

8. **Destroying the Image of Perfection in Man** – There is no perfect man except Jesus Christ. We don't point people to ourselves, but rather to Him.

9. **Free of What Others Think** – We recognize that we have a responsibility to be a witness everywhere we go, but we will not live our lives or do ministry,

in fear of what others may think. We will love the unlovable and reach out to whomever God leads us to or brings our way.

10. **Going There** – We will not be afraid to deal with whatever needs to be dealt with in order to become more like Christ.

Simply put, "Ministry with a mask-off approach is all about transparency."

BENEFITS OF TRANSPARENCY

1. When you become transparent, it will develop a closer bond between you and the people you are called to minister to. People will see you as approachable and will be less threatened by your spiritual stature. It will open the door for more meaningful ministry.

2. When you are willing to open up and share your weaknesses, as well as your victories, others will feel inclined to do the same.

3. Your transparency will allow others to realize that victorious, Christian living is not a life free from challenges, but rather learning how to trust God in difficult times.

4. When you become transparent you will allow the scriptures to be fulfilled;

   - Bear one another's burdens (**Galatians 6:2**).
   - Comfort one another (**2 Corinthians 1:4-7**).
   - Encourage each other (**1 Thessalonians 5:11**).
   - Forgive one another (**Ephesians 4:32**).
   - Care for one another (**1 Corinthians 12:25**).
   - Weep and rejoice with one another (**Romans 12:15**).

5. Most importantly, your transparency honors God. It will allow people to see that only God can heal a broken heart and restore broken dreams.

Regardless of where you are right now in your life, you need to know that God has a better plan for you. God wants you to experience His very best. You may feel hopeless right now or feel like you have blown your last chance. You may feel like your marriage is too far-gone, and you could never be used by God again. But God is still in the miracle-working business. If you will give God the opportunity, He will work all things together for good.

Romans 8:28 *says, "And we know that God causes everything to work together for the good of those who love God and are called according to His purpose for them." (NLT)*

About the Authors

Kendall and Starla Bridges are the Lead Pastors of Freedom Church in Carrollton, Texas, which over 2,000 people call their church home. Together, with their four children, two daughters-in-law, son-in-law and seven grandchildren (and counting), they serve and minister to the North Dallas community and beyond.

Contact Information:
Kendall & Starla Bridges
2435 E. Hebron Pkwy.
Carrollton, Texas 75010
972-307-2304
kendall.bridges@findfreedom.church
starla.bridges@findfreedom.church
www.bettermarriage365.com

Tim
" Healy in the Daily "
TimB

<u>5 Steps</u>

we All deal w/somedy!

SCAD -
Not symbl

He didnt
Help it

Made in the USA
Columbia, SC
09 February 2019